SCOTT FORESMAN

Art

Robyn Montana Turner, Ph.D.
Program Author

PEARSON

Scott
Foresman

Editorial Offices: Glenview, Illinois • Parsippany, New Jersey • New York, New York

Sales Offices: Parsippany, New Jersey • Duluth, Georgia • Glenview, Illinois • Coppell, Texas • Ontario, California • Mesa, Arizona

Program Consultants

Christopher Adejumo, Ph.D.
Associate Professor
　　Visual Art Studies
　　University of Texas
　　Austin, Texas

Doug Blandy, Ph.D.
Professor and Director
　　Arts and Administration Program
　　Institute for Community Arts and Studies
　　University of Oregon
　　Eugene, Oregon

Rebecca Brooks, Ph.D.
Professor
　　Department of Art and Art History
　　University of Texas
　　Austin, Texas

Sara A. Chapman, Ed.D.
Director of Fine Arts
　　Alief Independent School District
　　Houston, Texas

James Clarke, M.Ed.
Executive Director
　　Texas Coalition for Quality Arts Education
　　Houston, Texas

Georgia Collins, Ph.D.
Professor Emeritus
　　College of Fine Arts
　　University of Kentucky
　　Lexington, Kentucky

Deborah Cooper, M.Ed.
Coordinating Director of Arts Education
　　Curriculum and Instruction
　　Charlotte-Mecklenburg Schools
　　Charlotte, North Carolina

Sandra M. Epps, Ph.D.
Multicultural Art Education Consultant
　　New York, New York

Mary Jo Gardere
Multi-Arts Specialist
　　Eladio Martinez Learning Center
　　Dallas, Texas

Carlos G. Gómez, M.F.A.
Professor of Fine Art
　　University of Texas at Brownsville
　　　and Texas Southmost College
　　Brownsville, Texas

Kristina Lamour, M.F.A.
Assistant Professor
　　The Art Institute of Boston
　　　at Lesley University
　　Boston, Massachusetts

Melinda M. Mayer, Ph.D.
Assistant Professor
　　School of Visual Arts
　　University of North Texas
　　Denton, Texas

Reviewers

Studio Reviewers

Judy Abbott, *Art Educator*
Allison Elementary School
Austin Independent School
District
Austin, Texas

Lin Altman, *Art Educator*
Cedar Creek Elementary
School
Eanes Independent School
District
Austin, Texas

Geral T. Butler, *Art Educator*
(Retired)
Heritage High School
Lynchburg City Schools
Lynchburg, Virginia

Dale Case, *Elementary Principal*
Fox Meadow Elementary
School
Nettleton School District
Jonesboro, Arkansas

Deborah McLouth, *Art Educator*
Zavala Elementary School
Austin Independent School
District
Austin, Texas

Patricia Newman, *Art Educator*
Saint Francis Xavier School
Archdiocese of Chicago
La Grange, Illinois

Nancy Sass, *Art Educator*
Cambridge Elementary
School
Alamo Heights Independent
School District
San Antonio, Texas

Sue Spiva Telle, *Art Educator*
Woodridge Elementary
School
Alamo Heights Independent
School District
San Antonio, Texas

Cari Washburn, *Art Educator*
Great Oaks Elementary
School
Round Rock Independent
School District
Round Rock, Texas

Critic Readers

Celeste Anderson
Roosevelt Elementary School
Nampa, Idaho

Mary Jo Burkwocz
Wilson Elementary School
Janesville, Wisconsin

Mary Jane Cahalan
Mitzi Bond Elementary
School
El Paso, Texas

Cindy Collar
Cloverleaf Elementary
School
Catersville, Georgia

Yvonne Days
St. Louis Public Schools
St. Louis, Missouri

Shirley Dickey
Creative Art Magnet School
Houston, Texas

Ray Durkee
Charlotte Performing Arts
Center
Punta Gorda, Florida

Sue Flores-Minick
Bryker Woods Elementary
School
Austin, Texas

Denise Jennings
Fulton County Schools
Atlanta, Georgia

Alicia Lewis
Stevens Elementary School
Houston, Texas

James Miller
Margo Elementary School
Weslaco, Texas

Marta Olson
Seattle Public Schools
Seattle, Washington

Judy Preble
Florence Avenue School
Irvington, New Jersey

Tonya Roberson
Oleson Elementary School
Houston, Texas

Andrew Southwick
Edgewood Independent
School District
San Antonio, Texas

Nita Ulaszek
Audelia Creek Elementary
School
Dallas, Texas

Tessie Varthas
Office of Creative and
Public Art
Philadelphia, Pennsylvania

Penelope Venola
Spurgeon Intermediate
School
Santa Ana, California

Elizabeth Willett
Art Specialist
Fort Worth, Texas

Contents

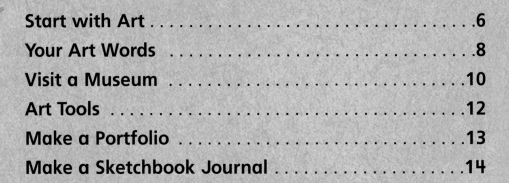

Unit 1

Art Around You 16

André Derain.
London Bridge,
1906.

Unit 2

Art Is Everywhere 50

Kenojuak Ashevak.
The Return of the Sun, 1961.

Unit 3

Art You Can Go Around 84

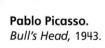

Pablo Picasso.
Bull's Head, 1943.

Unit 4

Creative Expression 118

Winslow Homer.
Breezing Up,
1873–1876.

Unit 5

Art of All Sizes 152

Artist unknown.
Firehouse Door.

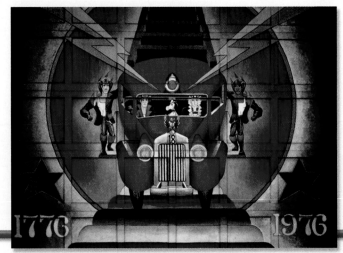

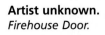

Unit 6

Types of Artworks 186

Katherine Westphal.
Unveiling of the Statue of Liberty, 1964.

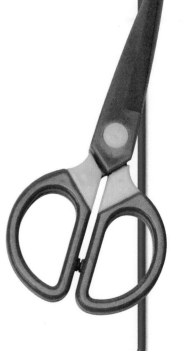

"A picture is worth a thousand words." You may have heard someone say this. It is a reminder of the power of art. Some art communicates beyond words.

Is it any wonder that the meaning of art is hard to explain?

Most people agree that:

- artists make art
- their works are called **artworks**
- artworks show ideas and feelings

Palmer Hayden. *The Janitor Who Paints,* 1939–1940. National Museum of Art, Washington, D.C.

Henry Moore. *Study for a Family Group,* 1945. Private collection.

Artists find inspiration for artworks in many places. Some artists show families in their artworks.

You are an artist. What ideas or feelings would you show in a drawing of a family?

Malcah Zeldis. *Thanksgiving.* Private collection.

Your Art Words

There are many words artists use to talk about art. You will see some of these art words in your book. They are shown in **yellow.** It is helpful to know these art words when you talk about art.

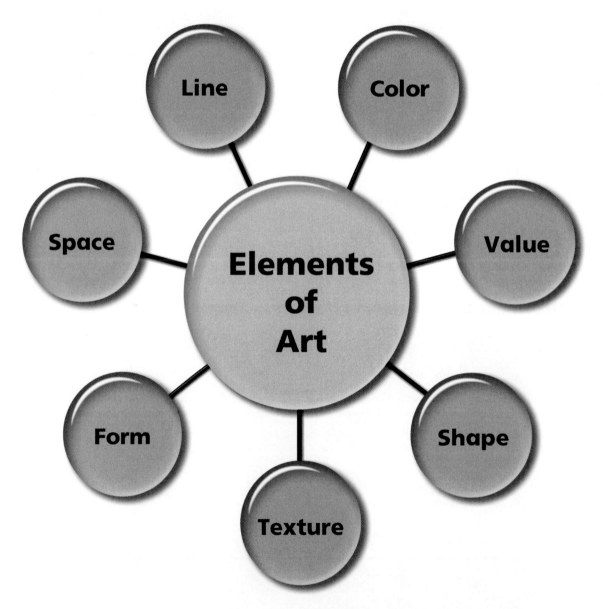

These art words name parts of an artwork.

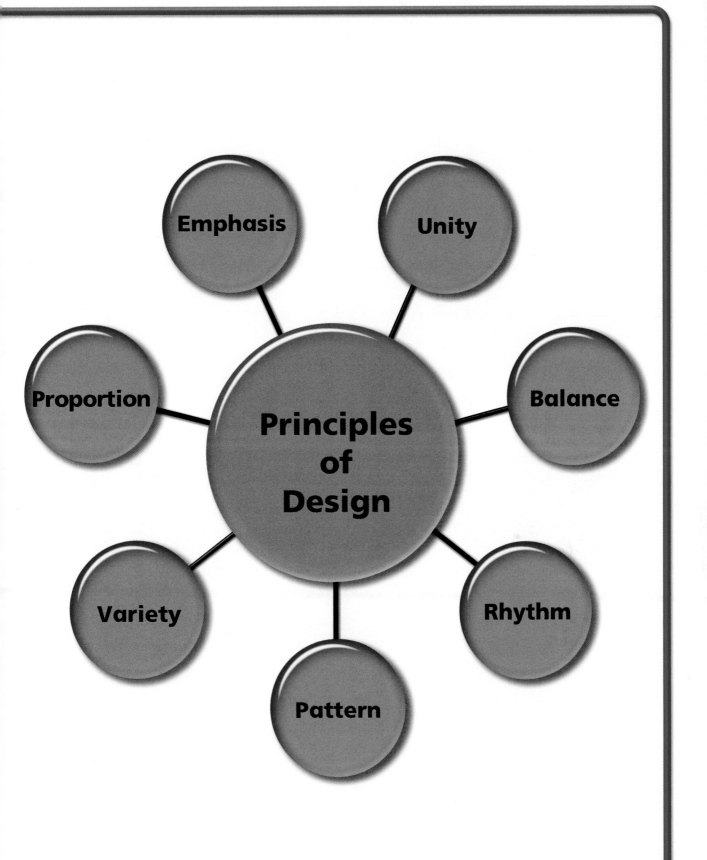

Emphasis

Unity

Proportion

**Principles
of
Design**

Balance

Variety

Rhythm

Pattern

These art words tell how an artwork is put together.

Rosa Bonheur. (Detail) *Rabbits Nibbling Carrots,*
1840. Oil on canvas, 21¼ by 25½ inches. Bordeaux
Musée des Beaux-Arts, Bordeaux, France.

Visit a Museum

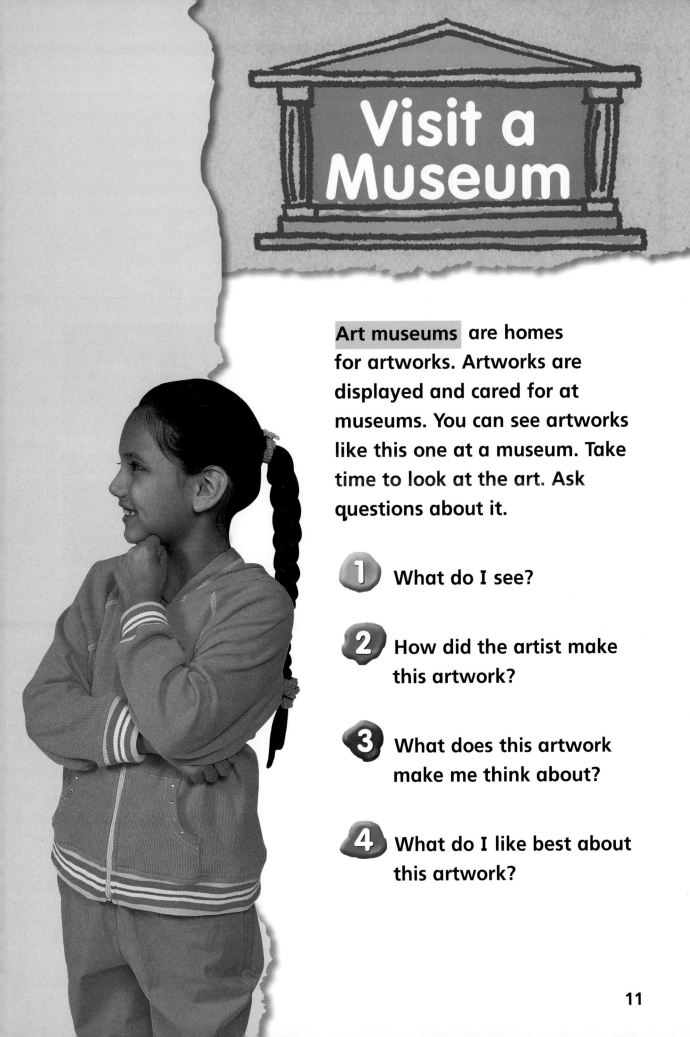

Art museums are homes for artworks. Artworks are displayed and cared for at museums. You can see artworks like this one at a museum. Take time to look at the art. Ask questions about it.

1 What do I see?

2 How did the artist make this artwork?

3 What does this artwork make me think about?

4 What do I like best about this artwork?

Art Tools

Artists use different art tools to make different types of art. You will use some of these tools as you make your artworks.

These tools are used for drawing.

These tools are used for painting.

These tools are used for cutting, taping, and pasting.

These tools are used for working with clay.

This tool is used for taking photographs.

Make a Portfolio

Artists often keep samples of their artworks in a portfolio. Follow these steps to make your own portfolio.

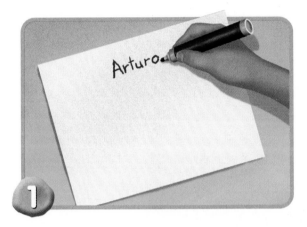

1

Use two sheets of poster board. Write your name across the top of one sheet.

2

Place one sheet over the other. Be sure your name is on the front.

3

Tape the bottom and sides together.

4

Use crayons and markers to decorate your portfolio.

Make a Sketchbook Journal

Artists often use sketchbooks to draw pictures or to write words about their ideas. A sketchbook is an art tool. A small sketchbook idea can lead to a much larger artwork.

Georges Seurat. *Seven Monkeys,* 1884. Conté crayon on white paper, 11³/₄ by 9¹/₁₆ inches. Musée du Louvre, Paris.

Follow these steps to make your own Sketchbook Journal.

1 Fold eight sheets of drawing paper in half.

2 Staple the sheets together along the fold.

3 Fold and staple a construction paper cover.

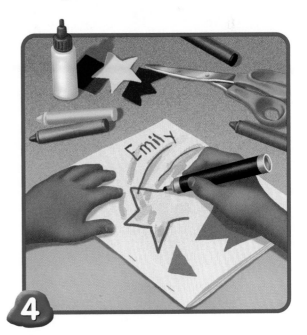

4 Decorate the cover. Write your name on it.

Mary Cassatt. *Children Playing on the Beach,* 1884. Oil on canvas, 38³/₈ by 29¹/₄ inches. National Gallery of Art, Washington, D.C., Ailsa Mellon Bruce Collection. Photograph ©1997 Board of Trustees, National Gallery of Art.

Art Around You

Some artists paint people they know or places they like to visit. They use line, shape, and color in their art. What does this artwork show?

Meet the Artist

Mary Cassatt was born in the United States in 1844. She spent much of her life painting in France. She is best known for her paintings of women and children. You can find another painting by Cassatt in this unit. What is that painting about?

Mary Cassatt. *Self-Portrait*, ca. 1880.

Line

A **line** is a mark that goes from one point to another. Lines can make waters look stormy. Follow the waves with your finger. Do you feel motion? How do these lines show action?

Katsushika Hokusai. *The Great Wave Off Kanagawa,* 1823–1829. Colored woodcut, 10⅛ by 15 inches. Metropolitan Museum of Art, New York.

curved

straight

zigzag

dotted

• • • • • • • • • • • • •

wavy

broken

—— ——————

spiral

continuous

Lines can be thick or thin. Some lines are straight. Curved lines go around. Zigzag and wavy lines go up and down. Find lines that are straight, curved, dotted, broken, and wavy.

What kinds of lines show waves in the storm?

Sketchbook Journal

Look for lines around you. Find three kinds of lines. Draw a rainy day with the lines.

Draw Different Lines

Use many kinds of lines to draw a school.

1 Draw an outline of a school.

2 Add trees, sidewalks, or other things.

Technique Tip

Use the tip of a crayon to make thin lines. Use the flat side of a crayon to make thick lines.

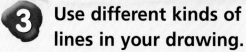 **3** Use different kinds of lines in your drawing.

4 Show motion by adding curved and zigzag lines.

Think Like an Artist

Tell about the lines in your drawing.
What feeling of motion did you show?

Shape

Sometimes artists use lines to make
shapes. What shapes are in this artwork?
Name the animals you see.

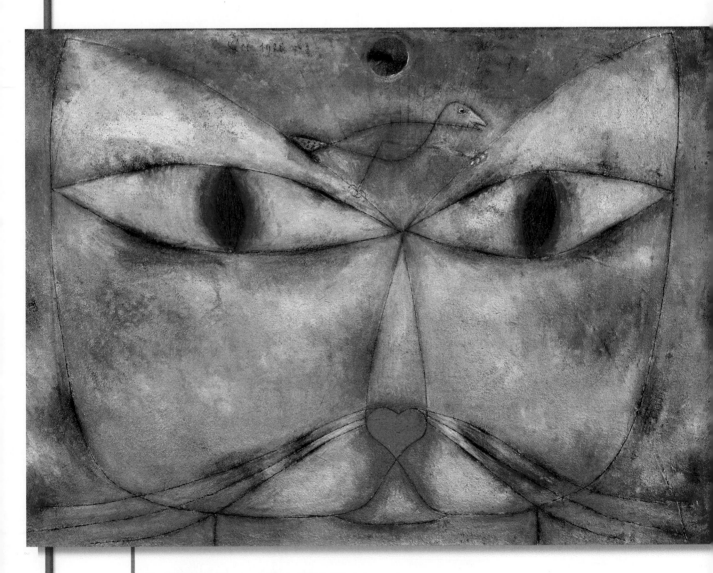

Paul Klee. *Cat and Bird*, 1928. Oil, ink, and gesso on canvas,
mounted on wood, 15 by 21 inches. Museum of Modern Art, NY.

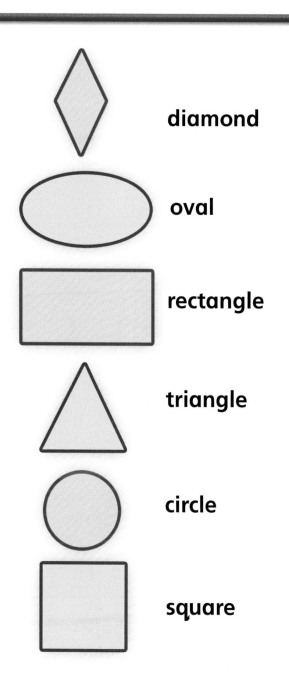

diamond

oval

rectangle

triangle

circle

square

Roberta Arenson. *Middle Billy Goat Gruff,*
2001. Collage, watercolor, and potato print, 9
by 12 inches. Collection of the artist.

Look at the shapes above.
Point to shapes in the **collage.**
A collage is an artwork made
of materials glued onto a flat
surface. What materials do
you think the artist used?

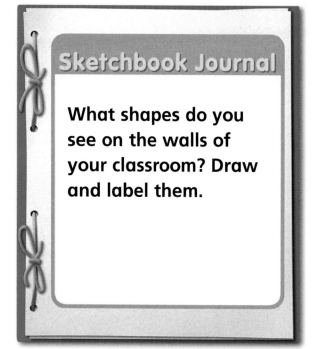

Sketchbook Journal

**What shapes do you
see on the walls of
your classroom? Draw
and label them.**

Studio 2

Make Animal Shapes

What are your favorite animals? Follow
these steps to make one out of shapes.

1 Cut out paper shapes.
Cut different sizes.

2 Arrange the shapes
to make an animal.

Technique Tip

Squeeze a little bit of glue in the center of
the shape. Dab a thin line around the edges.
Spread the glue with your fingers.

3 Glue them down.

4 Use crayons to finish your picture.

Think Like an Artist

Describe your animal collage to a friend.
Tell what shapes you used. Have your friend
guess what animal you made.

Feeling Texture

Texture is the way a surface looks and feels.
Texture can feel soft or hard. It can look rough
or scratchy.

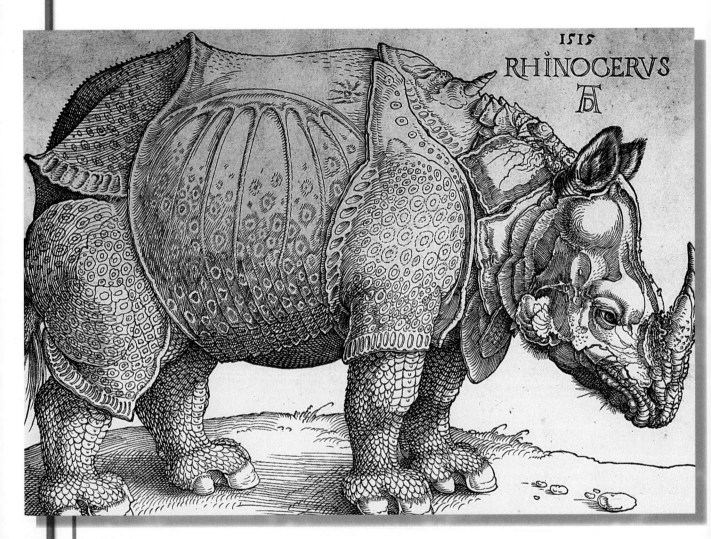

Albrecht Dürer. *Rhinoceros,* 1515. Woodcut, 9¼ by 11¾ inches. Prints Collection Miriam
and Ira D. Wallach Division of Art, Prints and Photography, New York Public Library, Astor,
Lenox and Tilden Foundation.

If you touch a rock, it feels hard. Other objects may have silky, soft, or bumpy textures. These are **tactile textures,** or textures you can feel.

Look at *Rhinoceros*. The artist used carving tools to show texture. What textures did he want you to imagine?

Art in My World

Look outside. Draw a plant or an animal you see. Show textures with lines and shapes.

Make a Texture Rubbing

Look around. Describe the textures you see.

1 Draw the outline of an object with large shapes.

2 Find objects with textures you like.

Technique Tip

To make a rubbing, place paper over a textured surface. Hold the side of a peeled crayon and gently rub the crayon back and forth.

3 Place a textured surface under your drawing.

4 Rub the side of a crayon inside the large shapes.

Think Like an Artist

Look at all the textures you used. Tell which ones you think look best. Explain your ideas.

River Scenes

André Derain. *London Bridge,* 1906. Oil on canvas, 26 by 39 inches. The Museum of Modern Art, NY.

The water in this artwork shows many textures. What textures did the artist want you to imagine? What lines did he use to create the textures?

Mary Cassatt. *The Boating Party,*
1893–1894. Oil on canvas, 35 7/16 by
46 1/8 inches. National Gallery of Art,
Washington, D.C.

What do you notice about
the texture of the water in
this painting? How is this
artwork like *London Bridge?*
How is it different?

Sketchbook Journal

**How can you show
textures in your own
artwork? Draw and
write your ideas.**

Seeing Texture

How would touching a real lion feel to your fingers? Your eyes can help you understand the texture of the lion. You can see **visual texture,** or how something seems to feel.

Rosa Bonheur. *The King of the Desert,* 19th century. Oil on canvas, 39 3/8 by 37 5/8 inches. Courtesy of Southeby's, Inc., New York.

Look at the objects in the photograph. Let your eyes tell about their textures. What are some words that describe the wall's texture? How could you describe the leaves?

Research

Find pictures of animals. Notice the visual texture. Tell how each animal might feel.

Studio 4

Paint Texture

Paint a picture. Use your brush to show texture.

1 Paint brushstrokes in one direction.

2 Wash your brush. Wipe it.

Technique Tip

Dip the paintbrush into the paint. Push down on the paintbrush for thick lines. Use the tip for thin lines.

3 Blot your brush.

4 Try a new color. Paint lines in another direction.

Think Like an Artist

What textures did your brushstrokes create?

Color Families

Look at the **colors** in the painting. Find yellow, red, and blue. They are the family of **primary colors.**

Stanton Macdonald-Wright.
Conception Synchromy, 1914. Oil on canvas, 36 by 30⅛ inches. Hirshhorn Museum and Sculpture Garden, Smithsonian Institution, Washington, D.C.

Color Wheel

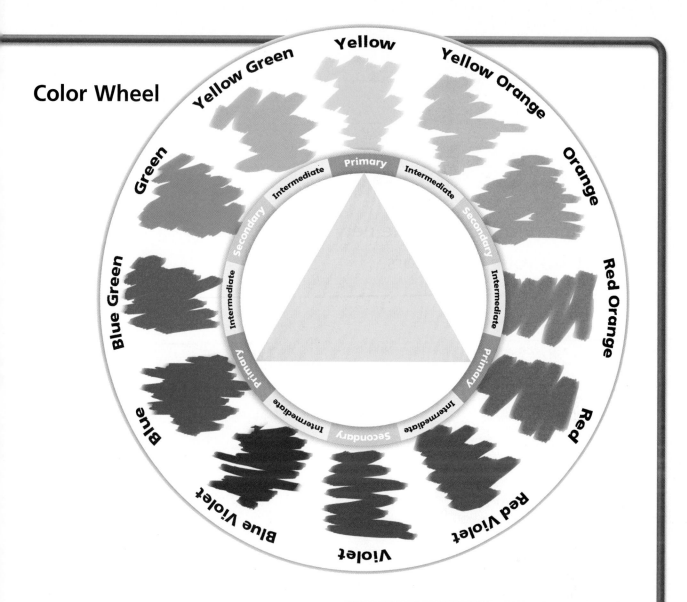

Green, orange, and violet are a family of **secondary colors.** You can make a secondary color by mixing primary colors. What two primary colors make green? orange? violet?

Look at the color wheel. Name the colors that form the **intermediate colors.**

Sketchbook Journal

Sort your crayons by color family. Draw and label the families. Match your color families with objects in your classroom.

Mix Colors

Mix primary colors to make new colors.
Paint with your new colors.

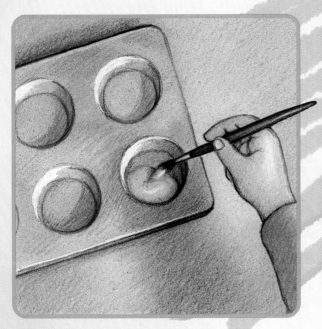

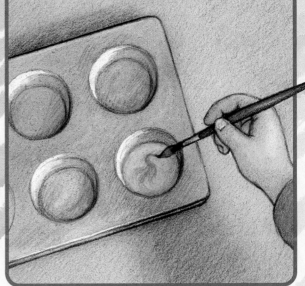

1 Put yellow paint on your palette.

2 Mix in a small dab of red to make orange.

Technique Tip

Choose colors you want to make. Use the color wheel to help you.

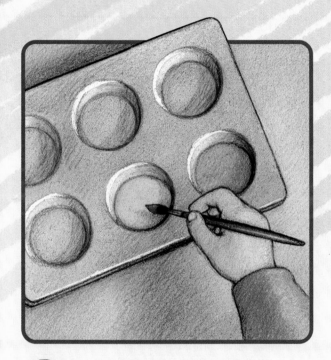

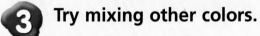 **Try mixing other colors.**

4 **Make a painting with the colors you mixed.**

Think Like an Artist

Artists experiment with colors. Tell how you experimented with paint to make new colors.

Warm and Cool Colors

Some artworks tell about feelings. Colors help show a feeling, or **mood.** What do you think the artist wanted you to feel about this painting?

Janet Fish. *Jonathan and Lorraine,* 1988. Oil on canvas, 64 by 72³/₄ inches. Abudefduf, Inc., New York.

Yellow, red, and orange are **warm colors.** Name some objects that have warm colors. What mood do the objects show?

Violet, blue, and green are **cool colors.** Describe a mood that cool colors show.

Sketchbook Journal

Use colored pencils. Draw two objects using cool colors and two objects using warm colors.

Make a Garden

Show a mood using warm or cool colors.

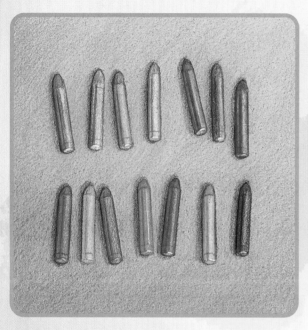

1 Choose warm or cool colors.

2 Draw a garden with oil pastels.

Technique Tip

Oil pastels have lots of color. Press lightly. Dab on a little color. Then smooth the color with a cotton swab or tissue.

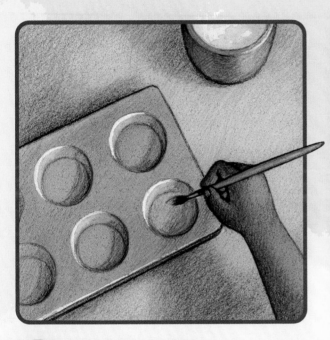

3 Choose a paint color for your garden.

4 Brush a thin coat of paint over your drawing.

Think Like an Artist

Think about the warm or cool colors that
you used. Tell the mood the colors help show.

Stained Glass

Sarah Hightower creates artworks from stained glass. She makes windows, lampshades, and other pieces.

Stained glass artists cut glass into shapes. Then they arrange the shapes and put them together.

Look at page 45. What colors do you see? What do the shapes remind you of?

Hightower says, "I feel that the glass reflects the way I feel about myself. I am strong, yet weak." What do you think she means?

Sarah Hightower cuts stained glass.

Sarah Hightower. *Mr. Bubbles.*
Stained glass and lead, 11 by 8 by 13 inches.

Sarah Hightower. *Fire and Ice.*
Stained glass and lead, 15 by 12 by 14 inches.

Make a Diorama

Make a diorama of your neighborhood.
Show people and places you find there.

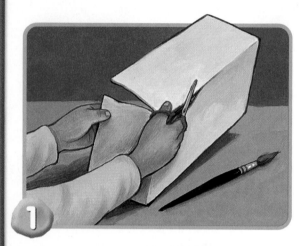

1 Cut away a side from a box.

2 Use cool colors. Paint buildings and plants.

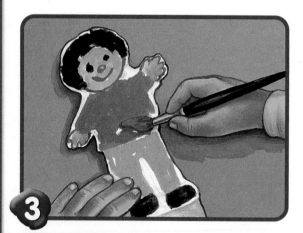

3 Use warm colors. Paint and cut out people.

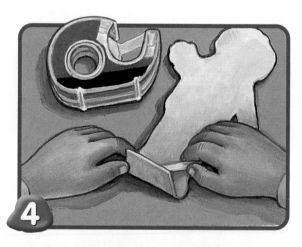

4 Make the people stand up.

Look at how these children showed
their neighborhoods.

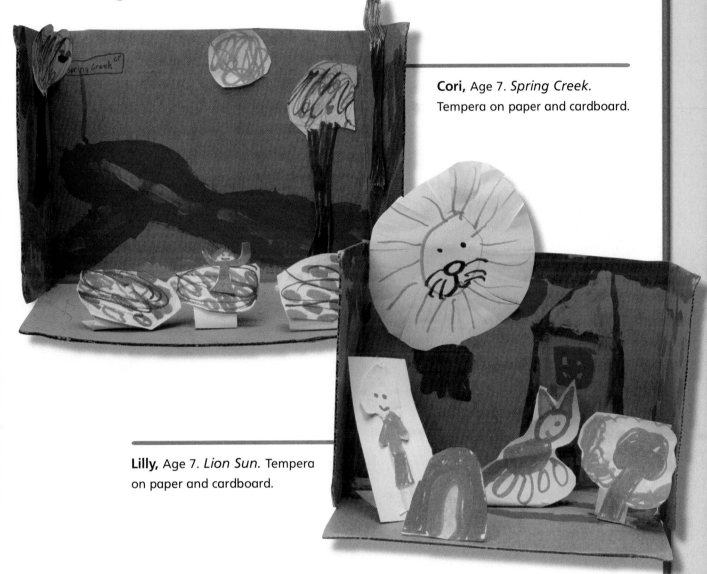

Cori, Age 7. *Spring Creek.*
Tempera on paper and cardboard.

Lilly, Age 7. *Lion Sun.* Tempera
on paper and cardboard.

Share Your Art

1. Point out some lines, shapes, textures,
   and colors you used.
2. Tell how you decided what things from
   your neighborhood to show.

Unit Review

Think About Art

Match the art words with the pictures.

line   tactile texture   warm colors

shape   visual texture   cool colors

Write About Art

Look at what a friend is wearing. Write about the textures and colors. Read your description aloud. Let the class guess who you wrote about.

Talk About Art

- Choose an artwork from your portfolio.
- Describe the mood in the artwork.

Joan Miró.
*Woman with Three
Hairs Surrounded
by Birds in the Night.*
Palma, September 2, 1972.
Oil on canvas, 95 7/8 by
66 1/2 inches (243.5 x
168.9 cm.). The Museum
of Modern Art, New York.
Gift of the artist in honor
of James Thrall Soby.
Photograph ©1996 The
Museum of Modern Art,
New York.

Put It All Together

1. What colors do you see in this artwork?
2. What do you notice about the woman's hair?
3. Read the title. What is Miró's artwork about?
4. What would you name this artwork? Why?

Fernand Léger. *The Construction Workers,* 1950. Oil on canvas, 118⅛ by 89 inches. Musée National Fernand Léger, Biot, France.

Art is Everywhere

Where can you find art? It is in many places. Look for art at home, at school, and as you play. Art is everywhere! Find line, shape, color, and texture in the things around you. What do you see that you think is art?

Dolbin. *Fernand Léger.*

Meet the Artist

Fernand Léger loved to travel and paint. Many of his pictures show people and machines he saw along the way. What machines are the workers using in *The Construction Workers*?

Find another artwork by Léger in this unit. Look for people doing everyday things.

Patterns and Prints

A **pattern** is repeated shapes, lines, or colors. You can find patterns in nature, in things people make, and in artworks. Which patterns are in this artwork?

Kenojuak Ashevak. *The Return of the Sun,* 1961. Stonecut, 24 by 36 inches. ©West Baffin Eskimo Co-operative Ltd.

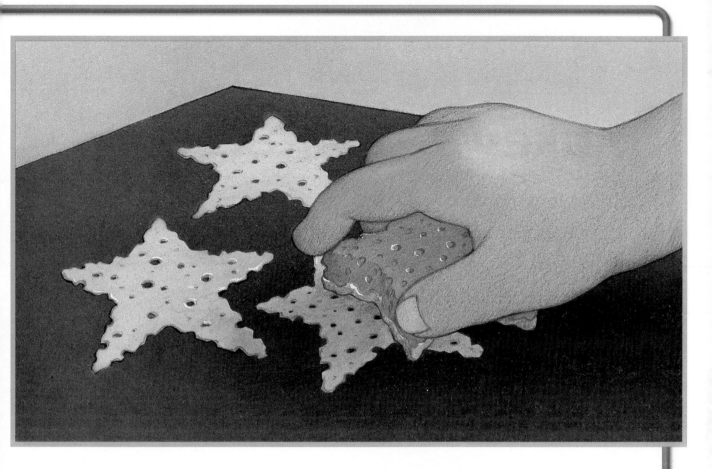

An Inuit woman drew the birds on page 52. To make a **print,** the bird patterns were cut in stone. Ink was placed on the stone and then the stone was pressed on paper.

There are other ways to make prints. How is the girl in the picture making a stamp print?

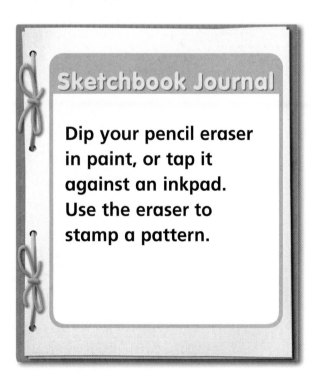

Sketchbook Journal

Dip your pencil eraser in paint, or tap it against an inkpad. Use the eraser to stamp a pattern.

Make Creature Prints

You can make a print with almost anything.
Follow these steps to make prints with your hand.

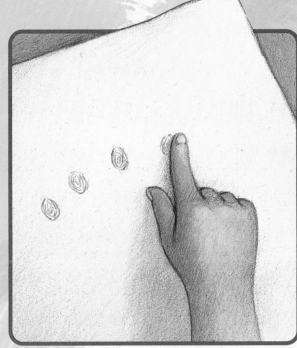

1 Paint your fingertip with a light coat of paint.

2 Press your fingertip against the paper.

Technique Tip

Press lightly when you print so the lines in your hand will show.

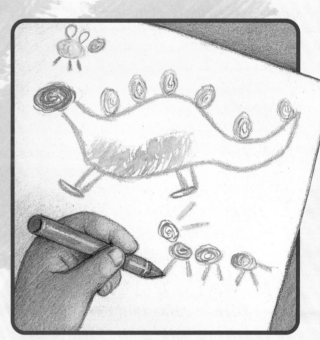

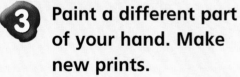

3 Paint a different part of your hand. Make new prints.

4 Add details to make creatures.

Think Like an Artist

Which print do you find most interesting? Why?

Another Way to Print

Look at this print. The same artist made the print on page 52. Did you notice how she used the same colors in both prints? What else can you say about this artist's **style?**

Kenojuak Ashevak. *Young Owl Takes a Ride,* 1984. Stonecut and stencil, 19½ by 25½ inches. ©West Baffin Eskimo Co-operative Ltd.

Amado Peña. *Los Pescados Peña (The Peña Fish),* 1978.
Serigraph, 22 by 32 inches. Courtesy of the artist.

The artwork above shows patterns with bright colors. The artist cut out stencils for the patterns. He put ink over his stencils. The ink printed onto the paper below to make a **stencil print.** Which parts do you think were made with a stencil?

Art in My World

Look for patterns in curtains, rugs, and clothes. Which patterns might have been made with a stencil?

Make Leaf Stencil Prints

Follow these steps to make stencil prints.

1 Fold a paper in half. Draw a leaf shape on the fold.

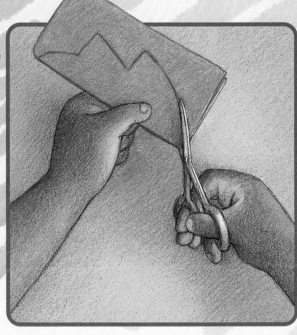

2 Cut out the leaf shape and set it aside.

Technique Tip

To cut out the leaf, gently fold it and cut into the fold. Carefully cut out the leaf shape to create your stencil.

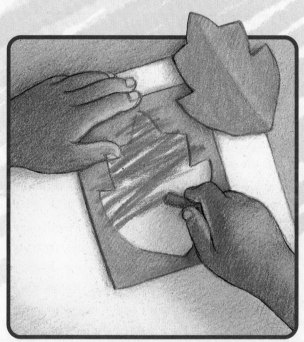

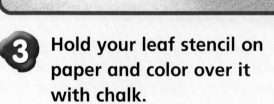 Hold your leaf stencil on paper and color over it with chalk.

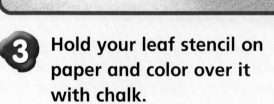 Remove the leaf stencil to see the print. Make other stencil prints.

Think Like an Artist

Tell what other materials you might use to draw and cut out a stencil.

Realistic and Abstract

The **subject,** or main idea, of this artwork is a squirrel. You might see a squirrel like this one outside. It looks real. This shows a **realistic** style.

Hans Hofmann.
Red Squirrel,
1578, Watercolor,
heightened with
white and gold
on vellum, 9⅞ by
7 inches. National
Gallery of Art,
Washington, D.C.

Franz Marc.
The Tiger, 1913.
Städtisches Galerie
im Lenbachhaus,
Munich, Germany.

What is the subject of this artwork? The style of Marc's *Tiger* is **abstract.** Most of the shapes do not show a real tiger. Yet, the painting may remind you of a tiger. Why?

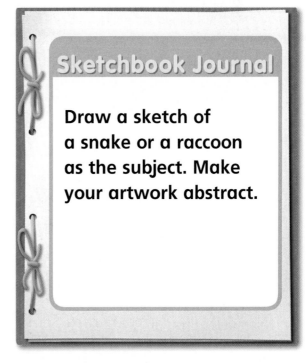

Sketchbook Journal

Draw a sketch of a snake or a raccoon as the subject. Make your artwork abstract.

Make an Abstract Collage

Think of an animal. Follow these steps
to show it in an abstract artwork.

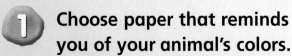 **1** Choose paper that reminds
you of your animal's colors.

2 Tear some shapes.
Glue them down.

Technique Tip

You may want to cut 2 or 3 shapes at once.
To do so, stack or fold the paper before cutting.

3 Cut a shape that looks like part of your animal. Glue it down.

4 Tear shapes from other colors to glue around your animal.

Think Like an Artist

Ask a friend to guess your animal. Talk about what reminds you of the real animal.

Look and Compare

Musicians in Artworks

Artists may paint the same subject. These two artists painted pictures of musicians. How are their styles alike?

Fernand Léger.
Three Musicians,
1944. Oil on canvas,
68½ by 57¼ inches.
Museum of Modern
Art, New York.

Pablo Picasso. *Three Musicians,*
Fontainebleau, summer 1921. Oil on
canvas, approximately 79 by 88 inches.
The Museum of Modern Art, New York.
Mrs. Simon Guggenheim Fund. Photograph
©1997 The Museum of Modern Art, New
York. ©1998 Estate of Pablo Picasso/Artists
Rights Society (ARS), New York.

Point out patterns in
each artwork. Describe
where you see them. How
are the patterns different?

Sketchbook Journal

**Draw two pictures
of the same subject.
Make one realistic.
Make one abstract.
Use patterns in both.**

Portraits

The picture on this page is a **portrait.**
The **expression,** or look on the person's face,
shows thoughts and feelings. What do you
think the man in this portrait might be thinking?

George Catlin.
*Big Elk, a Famous
Warrior,* 1832. Oil on
canvas, 29 by 24
inches. Smithsonian
American Art Museum,
Washington, D.C.

Alice Neel. *Sarah Greenberg,* 1967. Oil on canvas, 46 by 32 inches. The Estate of Alice Neel, Courtesy of Robert Miller Gallery, New York.

A young girl posed for this portrait. The girl was the artist's model. Look at the expression on her face. What do you think she might be feeling?

Sometimes artists use themselves as models. A portrait that shows the artist who made it is a **self-portrait.**

Art Fact

One artist, Frida Kahlo, painted over fifty self-portraits in her lifetime.

Draw a Self-Portrait

Be your own model. Follow these steps
to draw a self-portrait.

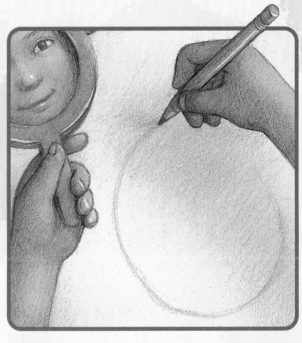

1 Look in a mirror.

2 Draw all of yourself
that you see.

Technique Tip

To draw with glue, hold the bottle like a
pencil. Hold the tip of the bottle just above
the paper. Squeeze lightly.

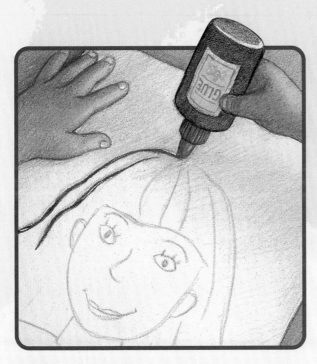

3 Go over your pencil lines with black glue. Let the glue dry.

4 Fill in the spaces with oil pastels.

Think Like an Artist

What shape is your face? Tell other shapes that you used to draw your self-portrait.

Still Life

This artwork is a **still life.** It shows objects that cannot move on their own. What did this artist use as models for his still life?

Paul Cézanne. *Still Life with Basket,* ca. 1888-1900. Musée d'Orsay, Paris, France.

Gabriele Münter. *Blumen in der Nacht (Flowers at Night),* 1941. Oil on cardboard, 20 by 26 inches. Hamburger Kunsthalle, Hamburg.

Flowers and vases can be models too. Look at the colors in this still life. Point to something blue.

Some blues are light, and some are dark. A dark color is a **shade.** A shade is made by adding black to a color. A light color is a **tint.** A tint is made by adding a color to white.

Sketchbook Journal

Plan a still life that shows your favorite foods. Make a list of foods you would paint.

Paint a Still Life

Think of subjects for a still life. Then follow these steps to paint them.

1 Mix tints of one color of paint.

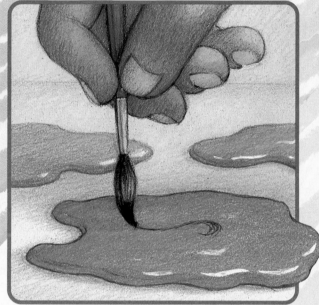

2 Mix shades of the same color.

Technique Tip

When you make shades, add tiny amounts of black at first. A little black goes a long way.

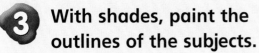 **3** With shades, paint the outlines of the subjects.

4 Use shades and tints to fill in your still life.

Think Like an Artist

How do you think the colors work together?
Tell which shades and tints you think work best.

Landscape as a Subject

Artworks that show an outdoor scene are
called **landscapes.** A landscape could show
a yard, park, forest, or a farmer's field. What
does this landscape show?

Henri Rousseau. *Virgin Forest,* ca. 1910. Oil on canvas, 44 by 63²/₅ inches.
Kunstmuseum, Basel, Switzerland.

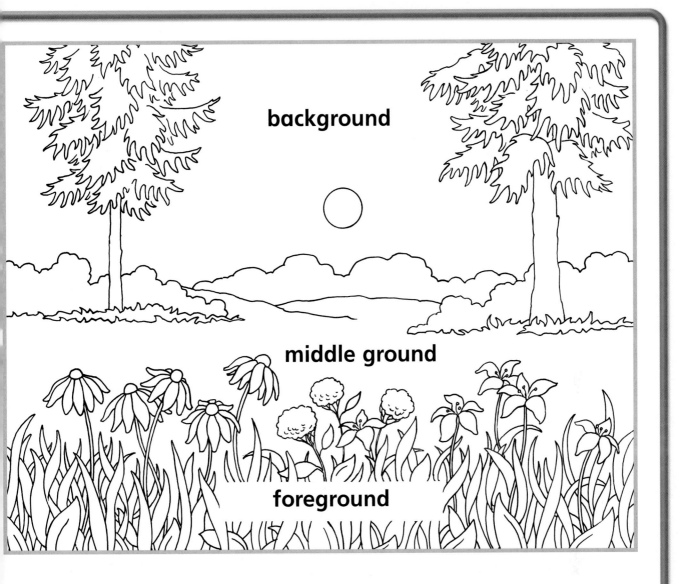

background

middle ground

foreground

In a landscape, objects in the foreground are bigger. They **overlap** parts of objects behind them. What objects are in the front, or foreground?

Point to a shape that looks farther away, in the background. Where do you see overlapping?

Research

Find landscapes in magazines. Study them. Look for open space. Look for plants that overlap other plants.

Build a Landscape

Think about what you like to see in a landscape.
Work with a group to make one.

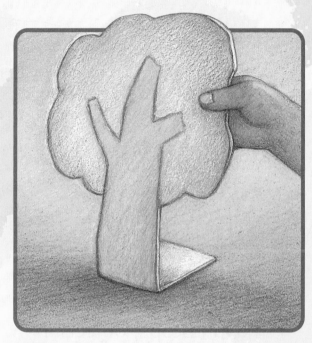

1 Cut out trees, flowers, and paths. Cut out a bridge or an animal.

2 Fold the bottom of each cutout. Make them stand up.

Technique Tip

Some cutouts may be too heavy to stand up.
Tape craft sticks to the backs of those cutouts.

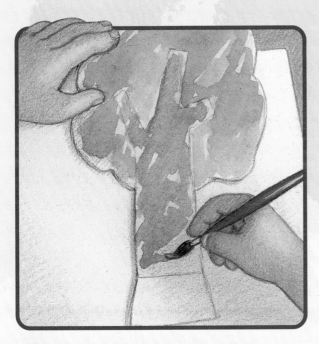

3 Paint your landscape cutouts.

4 Glue your cutouts onto a cardboard base.

Think Like an Artist

Look at your landscape from different angles.
Tell which things are in the foreground,
middle ground, and background.

Photographs

Keba Konte lived in San Francisco as a boy. He wasn't called Keba Konte then. He chose his new name on a trip to Africa. *Konte* means "storyteller."

Konte likes to tell stories. He tells them with photographs.

Konte's photographs are unusual. They are printed on wood instead of paper. When you look at the photograph, you can see the wood behind it.

Konte shows beauty through his artwork. He shows people and the things they do every day.

Keba Konte tells stories through his artwork.

Konte says this artwork "is about people, love, and struggle."

Print a Seascape

A **seascape** is almost like a landscape.
One thing is different. The subject is the sea.

1 Press hard on printing plates to draw fish and other sea life.

2 Tape handles to the backs of your printing plates.

3 Press your plates into paint and make prints on paper.

4 Paint a blue tint over your sea creature print.

Look at the seascapes these children made.

Mitch, Age 7.
Sea Shapes.
Tempera and
watercolor.

Abigail, Age 7.
The Sea.
Tempera and
watercolor.

Share Your Art

1. Tell if your seascape looks realistic or abstract.
2. Describe the hardest part of the project.

Unit Review

Think About Art

Read the art words. Then point to a picture that matches each word.

pattern	**abstract**	**landscape**
realistic	**portrait**	**overlap**

Write About Art

Look at the photograph of the landscape. What objects are in the foreground? Write about them.

Talk About Art

- Find a colorful artwork in your portfolio.
- Describe the tints and shades that you see.
- Explain why you like the artwork.

Franz Marc. *Yellow Cow,* 1911. Oil on canvas, 54³/₄ by 73³/₄ inches. Solomon R. Guggenheim Museum, New York. Photograph by David Heald. © The Solomon R. Guggenheim Foundation, New York. (FN49.1210).

Put It All Together

1. What do you notice about the colors in this artwork?
2. Where did the artist use tints and shades?
3. Do you think the cow looks happy or sad? Why?
4. What do you think of when you see this artwork?

Felipe Benito Archuleta.
Baboon, 1978. Carved and
painted cottonwood and
pine with glue and sawdust,
16½ by 42½ by 13 inches.
National Museum of
American Art, Hemphill
Collection, Smithsonian
Institution, Washington, D.C.
Gift of Herbert Waide
Hempill, Jr. and museum
purchase made possible
by Ralph Cross Johnson.
©1978, Felipe Archuleta.
Art Resource, New York.

Art You Can Go Around

You have made drawings, paintings, and prints. Each has a front and a back. But you can go all the way around this baboon **sculpture**. Just don't get too close to the big teeth!

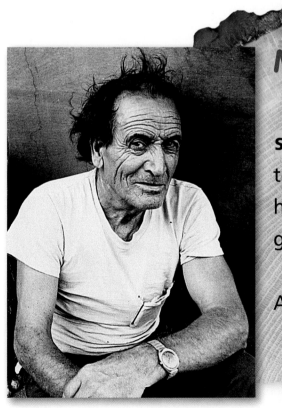

Meet the Artist

Felipe Archuleta was a **sculptor.** His first sculptures were toys for his grandchildren. Later he worked with his son and his grandson. They were artists, too.

Find another sculpture by Archuleta in this unit.

Forms in Places

A building is an artwork people use. It is an example of **architecture.**

Venturi, Scott Brown, and Associates. *Children's Museum of Houston,* 1992. Houston, TX.

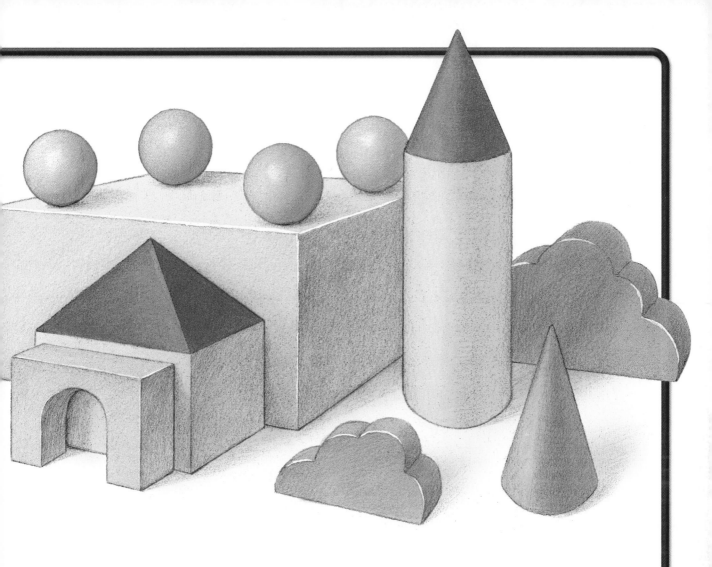

Builders and architects work together to make a building. Architects draw plans. Then they make a model. The model is a small version of the real thing.

The architect uses **forms** to make a model. Name the forms above.

Art Fact

Most columns are tall cylinders. But look at the building on page 86. Architects made some of the columns look like children!

Make a Museum Model

Think like an architect. Make a model of a museum.

1 Choose some cardboard forms.

2 Arrange the forms on a cardboard base.

Technique Tip

Secure each form with glue before adding the next one. When you add one, hold the shapes together and count to fifteen.

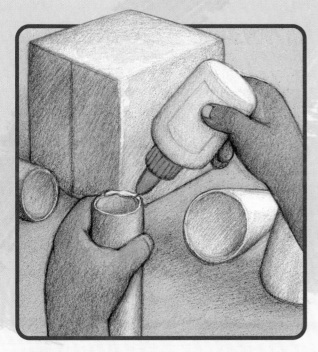

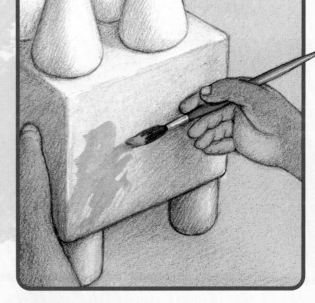

3 Glue the forms together.

4 Paint your model.

Think Like an Artist

Tell a friend what forms you used. Explain
why the forms look good together.

Playscapes

What do you like to do at a park? A **playscape** has forms to play on. Look at the playscape below. Name some forms you see. Which part looks like the most fun? Why?

Architects **design** playscapes. They begin with models. Architects make sure the playscape is safe and fun. Sometimes they ask children for help.

Look at the drawing. What forms would you add?

Art in My World

Where is your favorite playscape? Draw a picture of it.

Make a Playscape Model

Be a playscape architect. Make forms for a playscape.

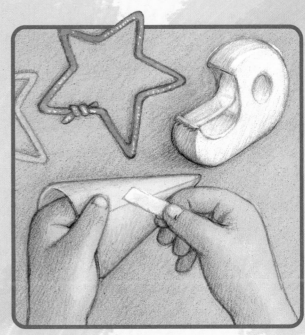

1 Cut and tear shapes. Bend and fold them.

2 Tape and glue them to make forms.

Technique Tip

To make a spiral, cut out a circle. Then start cutting on the outside edge. Cut around and around until you reach the middle.

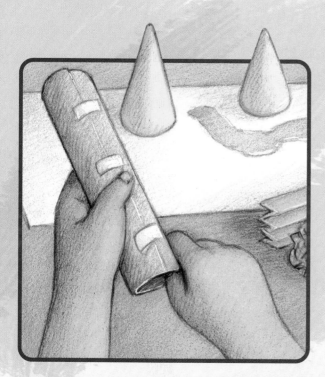

3 Arrange your forms to make a playscape.

4 Attach your forms to a base. Use glue, staples, or tape.

Think Like an Artist

What is special about your model? Where would you like to see your playscape built?

Forms and Space

Forms take up **space.** Look at the sculpture by Picasso. It is a form that you could go around. The space the sculpture takes up is **positive space.** What animal does the sculpture show?

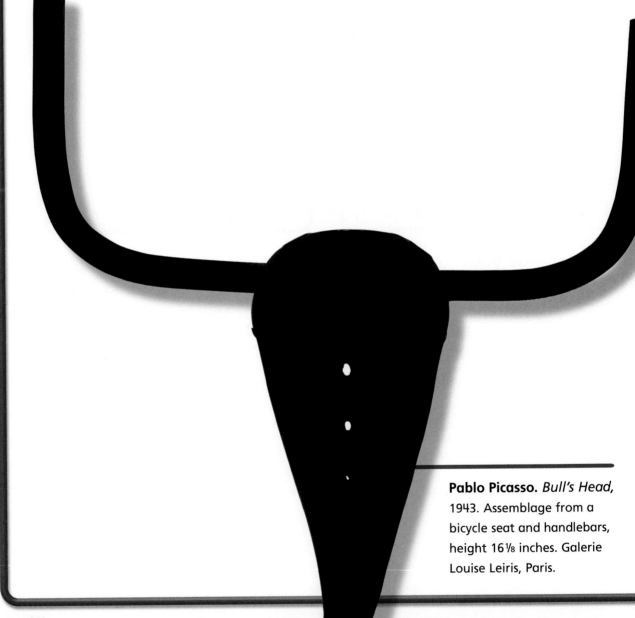

Pablo Picasso. *Bull's Head,* 1943. Assemblage from a bicycle seat and handlebars, height 16⅛ inches. Galerie Louise Leiris, Paris.

These sculptures are made from metal, too. Which sculpture is a bird? How can you tell?

Empty space around forms in an artwork is called **negative space.** Where do you see negative space in the horse sculpture?

Deborah Butterfield. *Woodrow,* 1988. Bronze, 90 by 105 by 74 inches. Walker Art Center, Minneapolis, MN.

Constantin Brancusi. *Bird in Space,* 1940. Bronze. Musée National d'Art Moderne, Centre Georges Pompidou, Paris, France.

Sketchbook Journal

Draw a sculpture made of metal kitchen tools. Use negative space around your artwork.

95

Make a Junk Sculpture

Even "junk" can become art. Make an **assemblage** by putting old metal objects together.

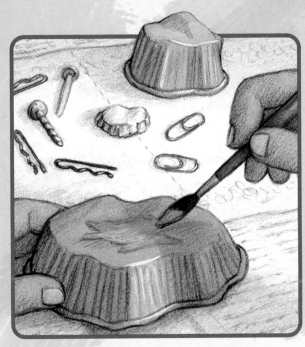

1 Gather small metal objects.

2 Add a little glue to your paint. Then paint some of the objects.

Technique Tip

Before painting, make the parts more interesting. You can bend and twist paper clips. Or curl wire by wrapping it around a pencil.

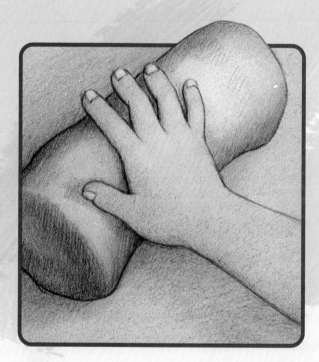

3 Make a base from clay.

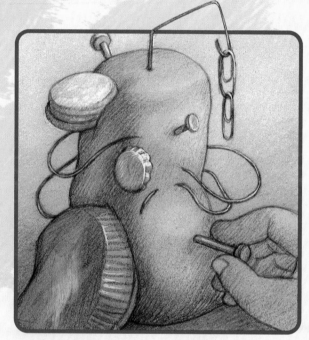

4 Put metal pieces into the base.

Think Like an Artist

Turn the base to view all sides. Tell
if your assemblage shows an abstract
idea or a design that looks real.

Animal Sculptures

Look at the tiger and the polar bear.
Both sculptures were cut from wood.
Point to the positive space in each.
Where do you see negative space?

Felipe Archuleta. *Tiger,* 1977.
Carved and painted cottonwood,
sawdust, and marbles, 35½ by 62¾
by 19½ inches. Smithsonian American
Art Museum, Washington, D.C.

Isaac Smith. *Polar Bear,*
1994. Painted wood, plaster,
22 by 49 by 22 inches. Collection
of Dr. Kurt Gitter and Alice Rae Yelen.

Look at the face on each animal. The faces show expressions. Are the expressions alike or different? Tell how they make you feel.

Sketchbook Journal

Which sculpture would you like to have in front of your school? Write a sentence to tell why.

Fun Sculptures

This toy looks like fun. The artist made it by putting together forms cut from foam flip-flop sandals.

Saarenald T. S. Yaawaisan.
Toy Helicopter. Recycled flip-flop sandals.
Museum of International Folk Art, Santa Fe,
NM. Photo by John Bigelow Taylor.

Artist unknown. *Horse Toy,*
ca. 1960. Painted wood, height 10 inches.
From the Girard Foundation Collection
in the Museum of International Folk
Art, a unit of the Museum of New
Mexico, Santa Fe, NM. Photograph
by Michel Monteaux.

This sculptor made
a toy horse in a different
way. He started with a
block of wood. He **carved**
the horse by chipping
wood away from the block.
Point to the places where
wood was carved away.

Research

People have carved
wooden toys for
thousands of years. Look
for pictures of wooden
toys made long ago.
Share your favorite one.

Make a Fun Sculpture

Collect art tools and materials.

Use them to make a fun sculpture.

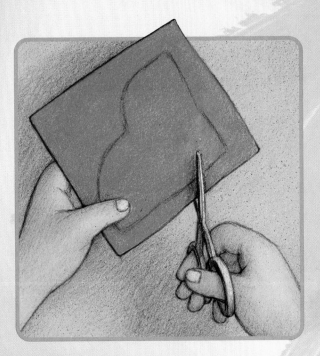

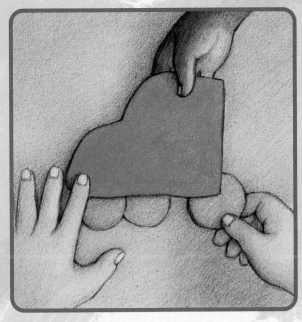

1 Cut foam into different forms.

2 Stack the forms to make a toy. Ask a friend to help.

Technique Tip

To use pipe cleaners, poke holes in the foam. Then push the pipe cleaner through the holes and twist the ends together.

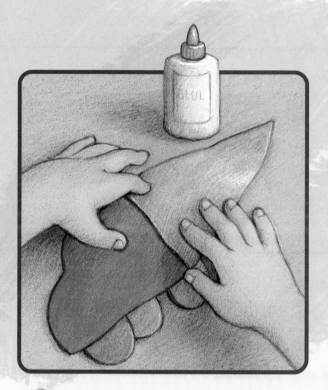
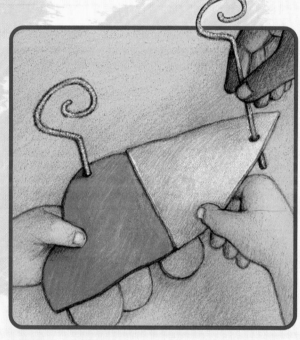

3 Attach the parts. Use glue, tape, toothpicks, or pipe cleaners.

4 Add new parts to your sculpture.

Think Like an Artist

How did your sculpture change as you added new forms? Are you surprised at the way it looks?

Puppets and Dolls

These **puppets** are about one hundred years old. They are made of wood and cloth. A **puppeteer** moves the puppets to tell a story. What story would you tell?

Artist unknown. *Marionettes: Sword Fighter and Dancer*, ca.1900. Painted wood and cloth, height 22 inches. From the Girard Foundation Collection in the Museum of International Folk Art, a unit of the Museum of New Mexico, Santa Fe, NM. Photograph by Michel Monteaux.

This doll is an example of **folk art.** Folk artists learn about art from other artists. Folk art often shows something about the artist's culture.

How are the clothes on this doll different from other dolls you have seen?

Artist unknown. *Burma Doll,* ca. 1960. Painted papier-mâché, height 10 inches. From the Girard Foundation Collection in the Museum of International Folk Art, a unit of the Museum of New Mexico, Santa Fe, NM. Photograph by Michel Monteaux.

Sketchbook Journal

Draw a puppet. Draw clothes to help people in the future see what your culture is like.

Make a Sock Puppet

You can make a puppet from a sock.
Use it to tell a story.

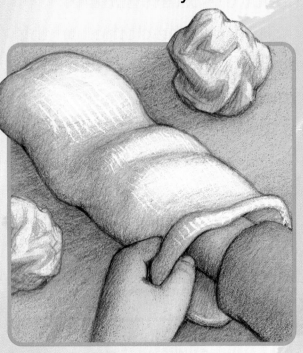

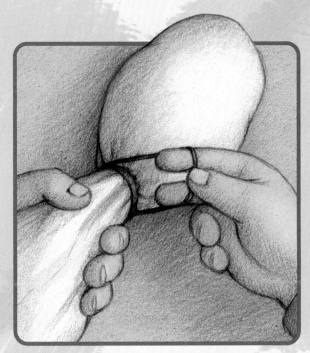

1 Make a head. First, stuff the toe of a sock with a wad of newspaper.

2 Then, wrap a rubber band around the wad of newspaper.

Technique Tip

Wrap paper strips around a pencil to make curls. The curls can be used for hair or jewelry.

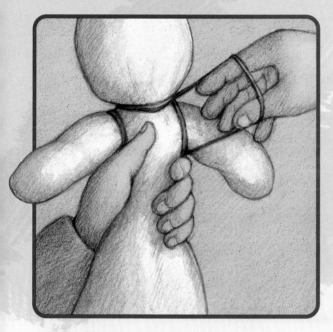

3 Make arms. Use wads of newspaper and rubber bands.

4 Add clothes, hair, and facial details. Use yarn, paper, and other art scraps.

Think Like an Artist

Artists use puppets to tell stories.

Move your puppet and make it talk.

What story will your puppet tell?

Pottery

Some artwork is made to decorate a space. Artists create other artworks to be used. The clay jar below is **pottery.** It is made to decorate and be used.

María and Julian Martínez, San Ildefonso Pueblo. *Jar,* ca. 1937.
Blackware, diameter 9½ inches, height 7¼ inches. The Heard Museum, Phoenix, AZ.

Josefina Aguilar. *Untitled (Frida Kahlo)*, 2002. Clay, height 28 inches. Private collection. Photograph courtesy CRIZMAC Art and Cultural Education Materials, Inc.

Artists who make pottery are called potters. They work with **clay** from the earth. Potters mold soft, wet clay into a form they like. They bake the forms in an oven called a **kiln.** The pottery gets hard when it is dry. Then the potter paints it.

Sketchbook Journal

Draw a pottery plate. Draw a design or pattern on your plate.

Make a Pinch Pot

Make a pinch pot with a design.

1 Roll clay into a ball. Poke your thumb into the center.

2 Turn and pinch the clay ball until you form a pot.

Technique Tip

You may want to carve patterns of lines and shapes onto the surface of your pot before you paint it.

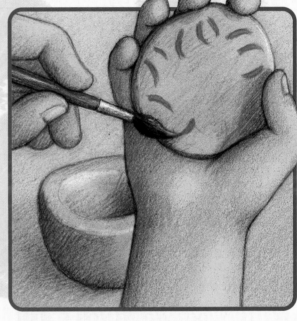

3 Make a lid from a flat circle of clay. Make it just larger than the top of your pot.

4 Let your pot dry. Then paint it.

Think Like an Artist

Tell a friend what you like about your pot.

Explain what you would do differently next time.

Plant Sculptures

Do you ever wish you could go inside a painting? Thanks to James Mason, you can.

In the late 1800s, Georges Seurat painted the artwork below. In the late 1900s, James Mason used the painting as an idea for his own artwork. Mason used metal and plants. He made large sculptures to show people and objects from the painting. He put the sculptures in a park.

James Mason is a sculptor. Most of his sculptures are made from wood, stone, or metal. But he also made sculptures from plants. What would you sculpt from plants?

James Mason

Georges Seurat. *A Sunday on La Grande Jatte–1884*, 1884-1886. Oil on canvas, 83 by 123¼ inches. Holen Birch Bartlett Memorial Collection, 1926. Photograph ©1996, The Art Institute of Chicago. All rights reserved.

James Masons sculptures add interest to this park.

Which figures in the garden can
you match to figures in the painting?

Make a Thumbprint Pot

Build a pot with balls of clay.
Use your own thumb to decorate it.

1

Roll small balls of clay. Then wrap a can in wet paper towels.

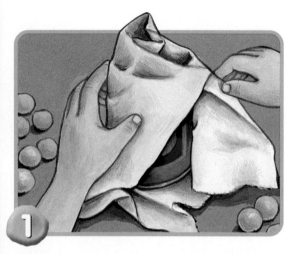

2

Make a flat clay base. Press the balls of clay onto the towels.

3

Remove the can. Carefully peel off the towels.

4

Let your pot dry. Paint it.

How did these children make the balls
on their pots stay together?

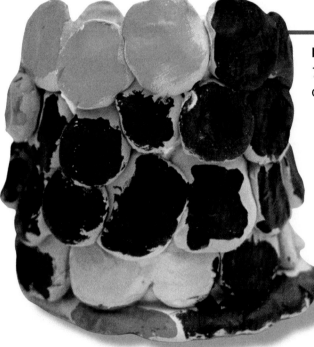

Lauren, Age 7.
Thumbprint Pot.
Clay and tempera paint.

Sophie, Age 7.
Thumbprint Stripes.
Clay and tempera paint.

Share Your Art

1. Tell why it was important that the clay balls
   touched the bottom and each other.
2. Suggest tips for others who try this project.

Unit Review

Think About Art

Match the pictures with the art words.
You may use the pictures more than once.

carve   positive space   puppeteer
puppet   sculptor   negative space

Write About Art

Write about the ideal playscape. Use the names of forms to describe it.

Talk About Art

- Choose an artwork you would like to revise.
- Tell a friend what you would change.

George Segal. *Walk, Don't Walk,* 1976. Plaster, cement, metal, painted wood, and electric light, 104 by 72 by 72 inches. Collection of Whitney Museum of American Art, New York. © 2003, George Segal/Licensed by VAGA, New York.

Put It All Together

1. Where do you see negative space in this sculpture?
2. Why are the people standing still?
3. What is the purpose of this sculpture?
4. Would you like to talk with these people? Explain.

Édouard Manet. *The Fifer,* 1866. Oil on canvas,
63½ by 38¼ inches. Musée d'Orsay, Paris.

Creative Expression

Creative expression is about sharing ideas and feelings. Some artists express themselves by talking. Some write or sing.

Visual artists express themselves through media. Some draw. Some paint or sculpt.

Look at *The Fifer*. What do you think this artist was trying to express?

Charles Emile Carolus-Duran. *Painter Édouard Manet,* ca. 1880.

Meet the Artist

Édouard Manet grew up in France. As a young man, he worked at sea. Then he studied painting. He used his imagination to paint. In his time, many young artists liked how Manet expressed himself. They tried to learn new ways to paint from him. Find another artwork by Manet in this unit.

119

Art and Music

There are many kinds of art. Music is art. Dancing and poetry are art. Storytelling is art too. What do these sculptures show? How do you think the artist made them?

Artists unknown. *Tang Dynasty Sheng Player, Dancer, and Panpipe Player,* 7th century. Clay. Royal Ontario Museum, Toronto.

Look at the whistle. An artist made it from **clay.**

One way to work with clay is to shape a flat piece called a **slab.** Artists cut the slab into parts and put the parts together to mold a form. Then they bake the dried form in a kiln to harden it. An artwork made in this way is called **ceramic.**

Research

Find pictures of musical instruments. Tell what they are made of. Describe the line, shape, and form.

Make a Slab Instrument

Think of your favorite musical instrument.
Then follow the directions to mold it from clay.

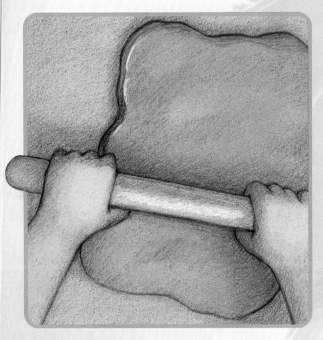

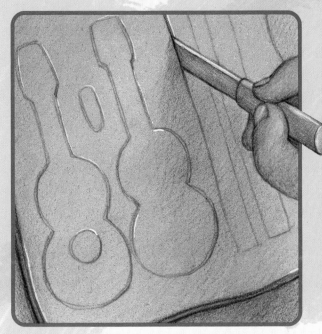

1 Roll out a ball of clay to form a slab.

2 Cut the slab into parts.

Technique Tip

Join pieces that you have cut from the slab.
Pinch them together at the seams and smooth
them with your fingers.

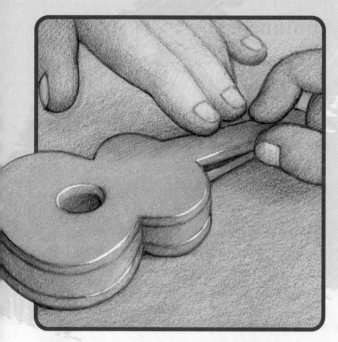

3 Bend and join the clay to make an instrument.

4 Add details.

Think Like an Artist

Do you think people might make toys or dishes this way? Tell why or why not.

Balance

Artists create artworks that show **balance.**
The pictures on these pages show types of balance.
The *Smiling Figurine* looks about the same on
both sides. It shows **symmetrical balance.**

Artist unknown. *Smiling Figurine,* ca. A.D. 6th to 9th century. Limestone, approximately 19 3/4 by 12 3/4 by 4 1/2 inches. Museum of Anthropology at Xalapa, University of Veracruz, Mexico.

Artist unknown. *Inlay of a king or deity. ca. 305-200 B.C. Opaque glass with gilding, 5⁹/₁₆ by 6 inches.* Brooklyn Museum of Art, Charles Edwin Wilbour Fund 49.61.1-4.

Artworks with **asymmetrical balance** have two different sides. Each side has a special part. Notice the tall hat and long nose on the king.

The pinwheel has **radial balance.** The lines and shapes move equally out from the center.

Art in My World

Go outside. Find objects from nature that show each kind of balance. Draw the objects. Label them.

Make a Coil Object

Create a clay object that shows symmetrical, asymmetrical, or radial balance.

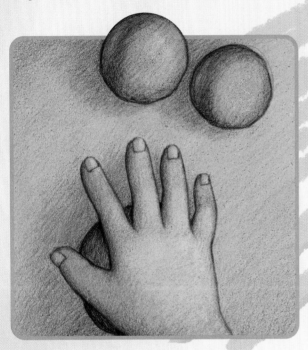

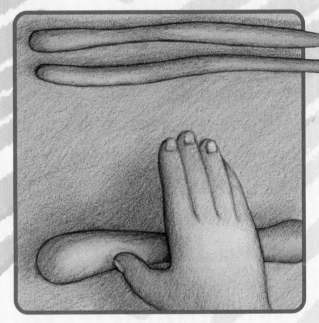

1 Form clay into balls.

2 Use your palms to roll each ball into a coil.

Technique Tip

To form a coil, begin with your palm in the center. Is one side thicker than the other? If so, move your hand to the thicker part and roll there to thin it out.

3 As you wind the coils, join them with slip. Then score the parts.

4 Add or carve away clay to make decorations.

Think Like an Artist

What kind of balance does your artwork show? Explain.

Lesson 3

Rhythm as Expression

The dancer looks like she is moving. Her **movements** show **rhythm.** Degas often showed rhythm as expression.

Edgar Degas. *The Star (Dancer on Stage),* 1878. Pastel on paper, 23 5/8 x 17 3/8 inches. Musée d'Orsay, Paris.

Repeated lines often create a feeling of **motion.** Which picture on this page shows fast movement?

Artists create rhythm to show movement. Look for rhythm in repeated colors, lines, shapes, or forms. Rhythm is a principle of design.

Sketchbook Journal

Look in a mirror. Watch yourself move. Then draw yourself in motion.

Studio 3

Make a Shadow Dancer

Follow these directions to create an artwork that shows rhythm and movement.

1 Draw a dancing figure. Cut it out.

2 Turn the figure over. Draw over it with white chalk.

Technique Tip

Lay the chalk on its side. Start in the center of your figure and move the chalk outward in every direction.

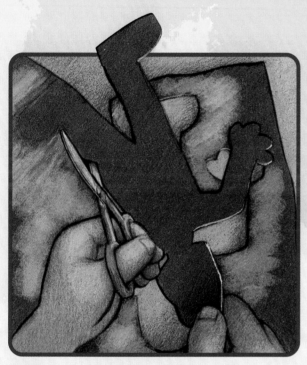

3 Set the figure aside. Cut out the dark shadow.

4 Glue the figure and the shadow to a light background.

Think Like an Artist

Tell how adding a shadow helps show movement.

Movement in Artworks

Which boat ride looks like it would be more fun? Which boat seems to be moving faster? How can you tell?

Édouard Manet. *Monet Painting in His Floating Studio,* 1874.
Bayerische Staatsgemaldesammlungen, Munich.

Winslow Homer. *Breezing Up,* 1873–1876.
Oil on canvas, 24⅛ by 38⅛ inches. National
Gallery of Art, Washington, D.C.

Talk more about what you
see in these artworks. Do you
think the artists were trying
to express the same ideas
about movement? Why or
why not?

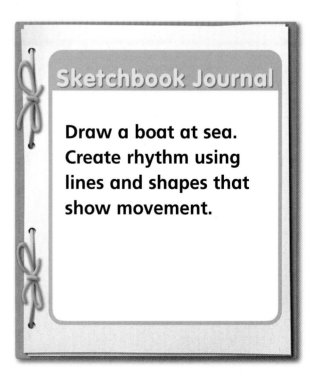

Sketchbook Journal

**Draw a boat at sea.
Create rhythm using
lines and shapes that
show movement.**

Unity and Variety

The artworks on these pages are alike, but they are different too. Name one way they are the same. What is one way they are different?

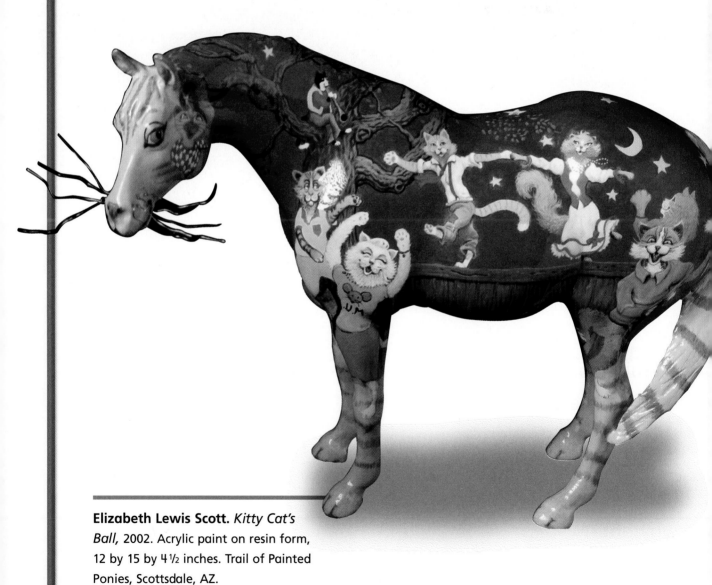

Elizabeth Lewis Scott. *Kitty Cat's Ball,* 2002. Acrylic paint on resin form, 12 by 15 by 4½ inches. Trail of Painted Ponies, Scottsdale, AZ.

Joel Nakamura. *Thunderbird Suite,*
2001. Acrylic paint on resin form,
5 by 7 by 2½ feet. Trail of Painted
Ponies, Scottsdale, AZ.

Bill Rabbit. *Earth, Wind, and Fire,*
2003. Acrylic paint on resin form,
7 by 9 by 2½ feet. Trail of Painted
Ponies, Scottsdale, AZ.

An artwork has **unity** when all the parts seem to go together.

Each horse shows unity. All of the parts work together to make a whole.

Look at all the lines, shapes, and colors. They show **variety.** They have parts that make them different.

Sketchbook Journal

Use one color to show unity in a drawing. Create the same drawing using several colors to show variety.

Show Unity and Variety

Follow these directions. Make a design
that shows both unity and variety.

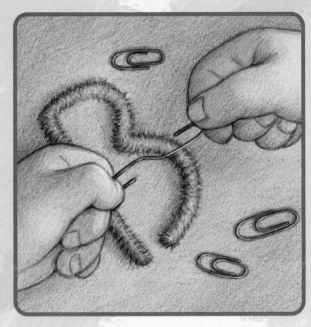

1 Think about ways to put
the materials together.

2 Bend the paperclips
and pipe cleaners into
different shapes.

Technique Tip

Some materials are glued together. Use
paperclips to help keep them joined until
they are dry.

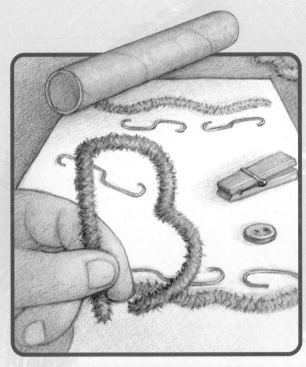

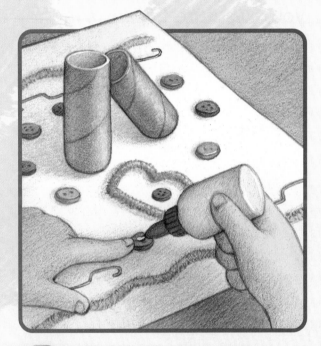

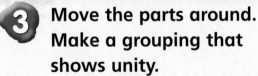 **3** Move the parts around. Make a grouping that shows unity.

4 Glue down the parts.

Think Like an Artist

Look at all the artworks together.
Tell how they show unity and variety.

Lesson 5

Proportion

Look at the cows. Which ones look far away? Which ones look closer to you? Measure the cows in the artwork. Which ones are bigger?

Rosa Bonheur. *Plowing in the Nivernais (Labourage Nivernais),* 1849.
Oil on canvas, 53½ by 104 inches. Musée d'Orsay, Paris. Photograph © R.M.N.-Gérard Blot.

Marc Chagall.
The Spring (Le Printemps),
1977. Oil on canvas, 36 1/4
by 28 3/4 inches. Christie's
Images, London.

Proportion is the size of an object compared to other objects. **Faraway** objects look small. Objects that are **close up** look large.

Look at the artwork on this page. Chickens are small, but this chicken looks big. Is it close or far away? The horse looks small. Where is the horse?

Sketchbook Journal

Look outside. Draw just what you see. Do not think about the real size of the objects.

Draw Proportion

Draw objects. Make them bigger or smaller to show how close or far away they are.

 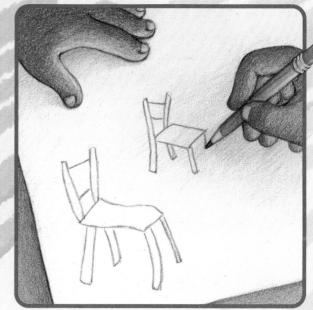

1 Draw the closest objects near the bottom. Make them big.

2 Draw objects that are a little farther away. Make them smaller.

Technique Tip

Nearby objects may seem to cover faraway objects. Overlap them in your drawing.

3 Draw objects that are farthest away. Make them smallest and near the top.

4 Paint your picture.

Think Like an Artist

Tell why you drew some objects larger.
Tell why some are smaller.

Symbols

This artwork was made in Mexico more than 500 years ago. A two-headed snake was a special **symbol** there. It stood for strength and wisdom.

The serpent is a **mosaic.** Small bits of stone were placed side by side and set in cement.

Artist unknown. *Double-Headed Serpent,* 15th century. Turquoise mosaic, 17 ½ inches. © The British Museum, London.

Robert T. Ritter. *Born Around the Campfires of Our Past,* 2001. Terrazo mosaic, diameter 40 feet. Floor of the Bob Bullock Texas History Museum, Austin, TX.

Mosaics can also be made of colored glass, paper, and other objects.

Recently, an artist made the mosaic above. It is on the floor of a museum. It tells a story about the history of Texas. What symbols do you see in this mosaic? What do they stand for?

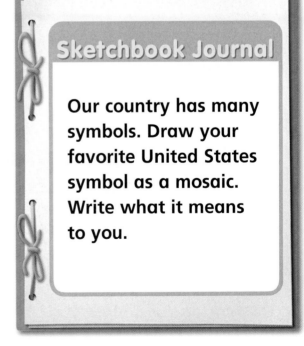

Sketchbook Journal

Our country has many symbols. Draw your favorite United States symbol as a mosaic. Write what it means to you.

Studio 6

Make a Mosaic

Make a mosaic. Show symbols that stand for your community long ago.

1 Tear paper into small pieces.

2 Draw a shape. Draw three symbols inside it.

Technique Tip

Leave a tiny space between each piece of paper that you use to cover the shapes and the symbols.

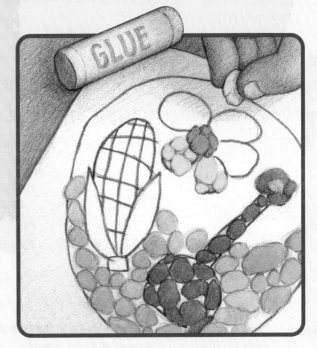

3 Cover an area with glue. Place paper pieces over the area.

4 Cover the shape and symbols with paper pieces.

Think Like an Artist

Show your mosaic to others. Tell them how your symbols support your ideas.

Window Displays

Good window displays do not just happen. Designers like Maribeth Koutrakos create them.

Koutrakos was inspired by her mother. The family moved often. Her mother decorated every home they lived in.

Koutrakos works to create the same feeling of beauty with her displays. She talks with the store manager. Then she draws ideas and plans what materials to use. She can use almost any object. Once, she used peanuts!

The goal is to catch people's eye. She knows she has done well when people stop and say, *"Wow!"*

Maribeth Koutrakos

Maribeth Koutrakos. *Baseball Locker Room*, 1995.
Window display, approximately 14 by 17 feet.

Maribeth Koutrakos turns things
we all use into window displays.

Make Symbol Prints

Think of symbols for the seasons, traffic signs, or feelings. Make stencil prints of them.

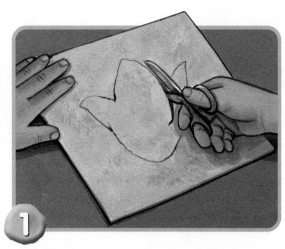

1 Draw a symbol on tagboard. Cut it out to make a stencil.

2 Roll a brayer in ink. Roll the inked brayer over the stencil.

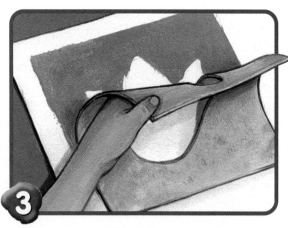

3 Turn the stencil over. Rub the surface. Then pull the print.

4 Repeat. As you work, think about how to show unity and variety.

What symbols did these children use in their stencil prints?

Ashley, Age 7. *Heartbeats.* Tempera on construction paper.

Ashley Nicole, Age 8. *Star.* Tempera on construction paper.

Share Your Art

1. What is your print about? Why did you choose that symbol?
2. Explain how you showed unity and variety.

Unit Review

Think About Art

Match the pictures with the art words.

radial balance   **movement**   **unity**

mosaic   **rhythm**   **variety**

Write About Art

Draw a symbol to express an idea about yourself. Write about why you chose the symbol.

Talk About Art

- Choose an artwork from your portfolio.
- What kind of balance does the artwork show?
- Tell a friend. Explain how you know.

Auguste Rodin. *The Thinker,*
1880. Bronze, approximately
72 by 39⅕ by 58 inches. © Rodin
Museum, Paris. Photograph
© 1995 AKG London/Justus Göpel.

Put It All Together

1. What type of balance does this sculpture have?
2. What idea do you think the artist is expressing?
3. Do you think this sculpture has unity? Explain.
4. Where might be a good place to set
   this sculpture? Why?

Alexander Calder. *Little Spider,* ca. 1940.
Painted sheet metal and wire, 55 by 50
inches. National Gallery of Art, gift of
Mr. and Mrs. Klaus G. Perls (1996.120.18).
© 2000 Estate of Alexander Calder/Artists
Rights Society (ARS), New York.

Art of All Sizes

Artworks come in all sizes. Some are big and some are small. Some artworks are about the same size as their subjects, but most are not.

The artwork on page 152 is called *Little Spider.* But this spider is not so little! It is about four feet tall and five feet long.

Meet the Artist

Alexander Calder studied to be an engineer. Then he went to art school. One of his first sculptures was a tiny circus. Calder went on to make artworks of all sizes. His huge sculptures can be found in cities all over the world. Find another sculpture by Calder in this unit.

Large Sculptures

This large sculpture shows characters created by Dr. Seuss. It is an outdoor sculpture. Which characters do you see?

Lark Grey Dimond-Cates. Dr. Seuss and the Cat in the Hat, at the Dr. Seuss National Memorial Sculpture Garden, Springfield, MA.

Claes Oldenburg and Coosje van Bruggen. (Detail) *Bicyclette Ensevelié (Buried Bicycle),* 1990.

These artworks are called **public sculptures.** They are large so that many people can enjoy them at the same time.

You may see public sculptures in parks or in other busy places. They often show familiar objects. What does the sculpture on this page show?

Art in My World

Think about a public sculpture that is in your community. Draw it. Tell what it is. Tell where you saw it.

Make a Sculpture Garden

Work with a group to make a sculpture garden. Show your favorite story characters.

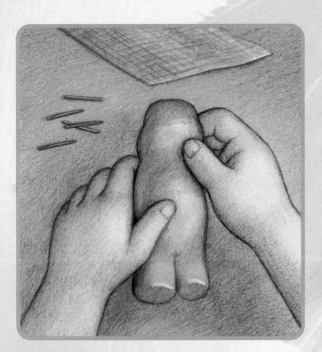

1 Make book characters from modeling clay.

2 Add texture and detail to your sculpture.

Technique Tip

To join clay pieces, press and blend them together with your fingers.

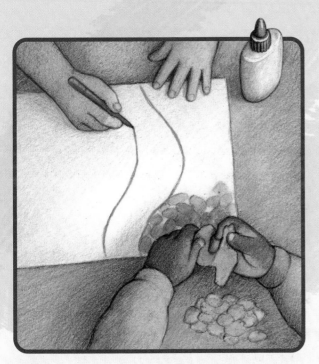

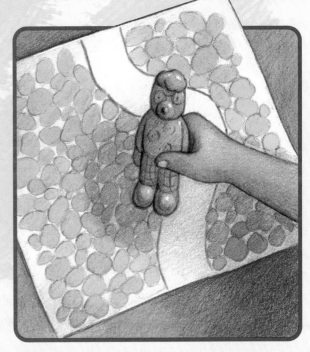

3 Work with your group to make a base.

4 Arrange the characters on the base.

Think Like an Artist

Suppose that your sculpture garden is real.
Do you think it would be fun to play in?
Describe what you would do there.

Artists Paint Murals

This artwork is a **mural.** A mural is a large painting on a wall, ceiling, fence, floor, or door. This mural is called *Firehouse Door.* What do you think is behind the door?

Artist unknown. *Firehouse Door,* West Village, New York, NY.

Murals like *Firehouse Door* show a **realistic** style. They show scenes that look real. Some murals show scenes that are not real. They have an **imaginary** style. Many murals tell stories.

The children on this page are creating a mural. Does their mural show a realistic or imaginary style? What story might it be telling?

Sketchbook Journal

Draw the main parts of a mural that you would like to create. Tell where you would paint the mural.

Studio 2

Make a Mural

Work with friends to make a mural. Make it show a realistic or an imaginary style.

1 Plan the mural together.

2 Paint a background together.

Technique Tip

Use large paintbrushes to paint most of the background. Use small brushes for details.

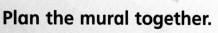

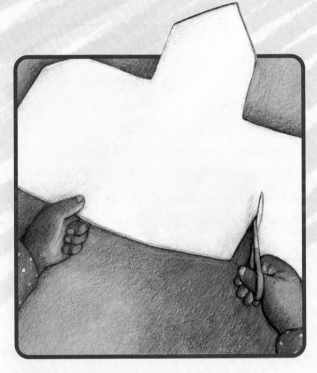

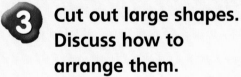 **Cut out large shapes. Discuss how to arrange them.**

4 **Glue the large shapes onto the mural.**

Think Like an Artist

Tell what your mural shows. Tell if it has a realistic or an imaginary style.

Small Symbols

The next time you get a letter, look at the stamp on it. **Postage stamps** are tiny prints of larger artworks. Some stamps have designs of events in our country's history.

FIRST FLIGHT · WRIGHT BROTHERS · 1903
2003

McRay Magleby. *First Flight • Wright Brothers • 1903,* 2003.
Computer-generated design for a U.S. postage stamp. © 2003 USPS.

Lance Hidy. *Special Olympics,* 2003. Computer-generated design for a U.S. postage stamp. © 2003 USPS.

Michael Osborne. *LOVE,* 2002. Computer-generated design for a U.S. postage stamp. © 2003 USPS.

The postage stamps on this page have something in common. Each one has a **symbol** on it. The symbol stands for a real object or an idea. Point to the heart on the second stamp. The heart stands for love. What symbols do you see on the other stamp? What might the symbols stand for?

Art in My World

Collect postage stamps. Tell a story about your favorite tiny artwork.

163

Design a Stamp

Follow these steps to design a postage stamp.
Be sure to use symbols for main ideas.

1 Draw a symbol that is important to you.

2 Cut paper shapes to make the symbol.

Technique Tip

You may want to overlap some of the cutouts. Then glue the cutouts, one at a time, to the card. Use only a small amount of glue or your stamp will wrinkle.

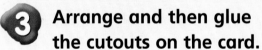 **3** **Arrange and then glue the cutouts on the card.**

4 **Cut around the edges to make it look like a stamp.**

Think Like an Artist

Tell a story about your stamp.

Explain what the symbol stands for.

Look and Compare

Large and Small Artworks

Alexander Calder. *Cheval Rouge (Red Horse),* 1974. Sheet metal and paint, approximately 16 by 19 by 19 feet. Private collection.

Alexander Calder made both of these artworks. One is large and one is very small. What is the subject of each artwork? What do you think each symbol stands for?

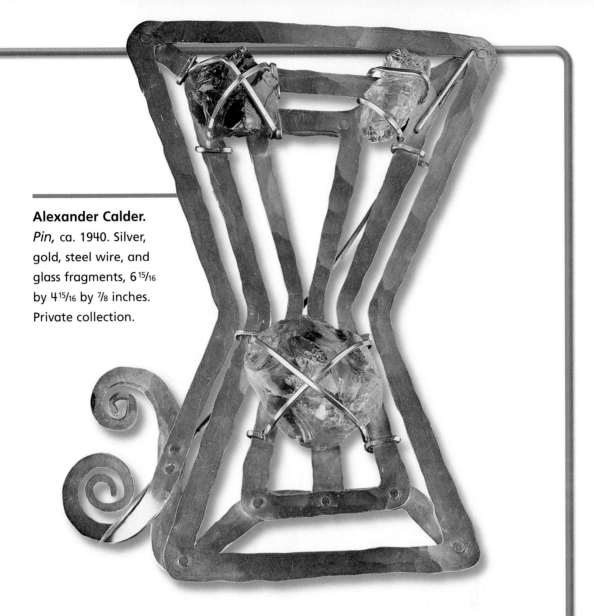

Alexander Calder.
Pin, ca. 1940. Silver,
gold, steel wire, and
glass fragments, 6¹⁵/₁₆
by 4¹⁵/₁₆ by ⅞ inches.
Private collection.

Did Calder use a
realistic or an imaginary
style? Explain.

Look at the lines in
both artworks. Point to the
straight lines. What other
kinds of lines do you see?

Which is your favorite
artwork? Why?

Art in My World

You could wear the
artwork on this page.
Draw an artwork
that you have seen
someone wear.

Emphasis in Jewelry

Jewelry is art that is small enough to wear. Look at the **pendant** that is hanging from this necklace of tradebeads. It is small, but it gets your attention!

Artist unknown, Moroccan.
Berber Necklace. Beads, metalwork, and inlaid precious stones. Photograph © Francesco Venturi/CORBIS.

Artist unknown. *Papayan (Columbian) Pectoral,* A.D. 1100–1500. Cast gold-copper alloy, gilded, height 11 3/4 inches. © The British Museum, London.

Artists often give importance, or **emphasis,** to one part of an artwork. They use color, size, shape, or placement to make you look.

The pendant on this page is very old. Someone wore it long ago as part of a necklace. Point to the part that shows emphasis.

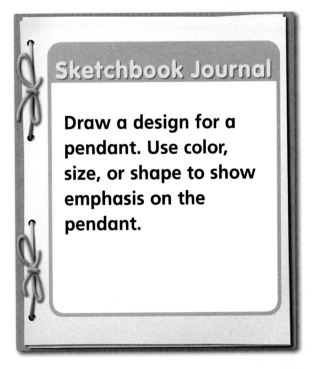

Sketchbook Journal

Draw a design for a pendant. Use color, size, or shape to show emphasis on the pendant.

169

Make Tradebeads

Make beads to trade with friends. Use them to make a necklace with a pendant.

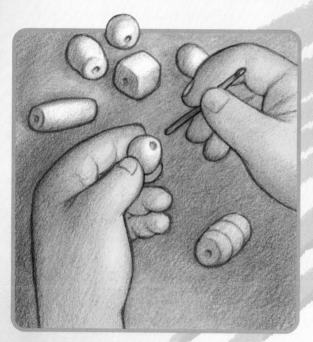

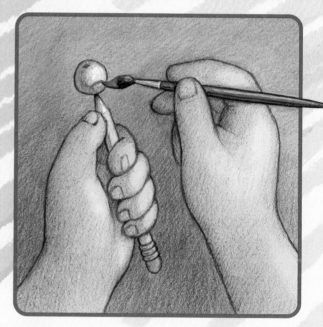

1 Make small clay forms. Make a hole in each form. Let them dry.

2 Paint patterns with lines and shapes. Trade the dried beads.

Technique Tip

Do not make the holes in your beads and pendant too small. The holes will shrink as they dry.

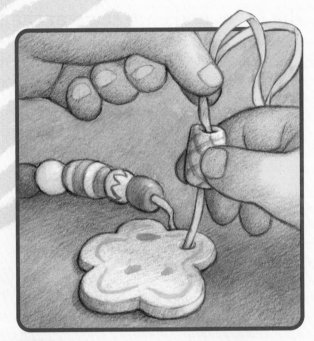

3 Cut a pendant from clay. Poke a hole in it and let it dry. Paint it.

4 String the beads and your pendant to make a necklace.

Think Like an Artist

Did you like trading the beads? Explain. Tell which beads on your necklace show emphasis.

Artists Design Books

Look at all the lines, colors, and shapes on this book cover! A **book designer** planned how the cover and each page of the book would look.

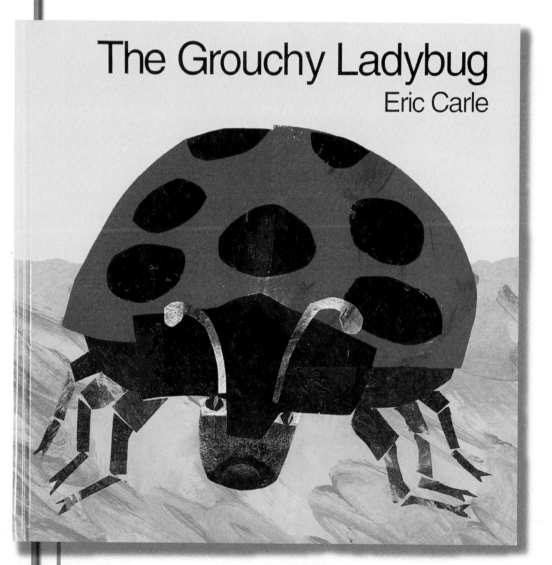

The Grouchy Ladybug
Eric Carle

Eric Carle. Cover of *The Grouchy Ladybug,* by Eric Carle, 1977. Harper Collins Publishers.

Book designers often use computers to design books. They choose a style for the letters and words. They choose pictures and decide how to fill the space on the pages.

Some book designers use **computer art.** They use computer software to create artworks. What other tools do they need?

Sketchbook Journal

Draw a computer screen. Draw art on the screen to show something you would like to draw on the computer.

Make a Zigzag Book

Design pages about your favorite school subject or activity to make a zigzag book.

1 Make designs for the front and back covers.

2 Fold a long paper to make the book pages.

Technique Tip

Use a template to mark where your folds should be. Fold the paper on the marks. Fold it like a big fan.

3 Draw a design for each book page.

4 Glue the folded paper to the front and back covers.

Think Like an Artist

Tell how you might use a computer to design your book.

Artists Make Miniatures

You can hold this fancy egg in your hand. But look inside. Surprise! When you open the egg, a tiny palace appears. It is a model of a real palace in Russia. A tiny model is called a **miniature.**

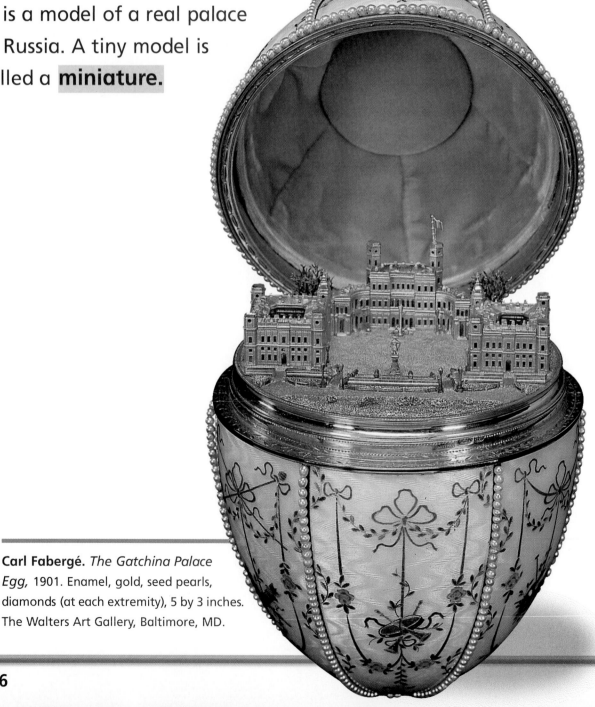

Carl Fabergé. *The Gatchina Palace Egg,* 1901. Enamel, gold, seed pearls, diamonds (at each extremity), 5 by 3 inches. The Walters Art Gallery, Baltimore, MD.

Gatchina Palace

Look at the design on the outside of the egg. The lines in the design lead your eye to the palace.

Now look at the picture of the real palace. Where did the architect show emphasis?

Make a Surprise Egg

Decorate an egg that will hide a clay surprise.

1 Draw an egg shape. Show a surprise in the egg.

2 Decorate a plastic egg. Glue objects to the outside.

Technique Tip

Work slowly. Let the glue dry before adding each new object to the egg.

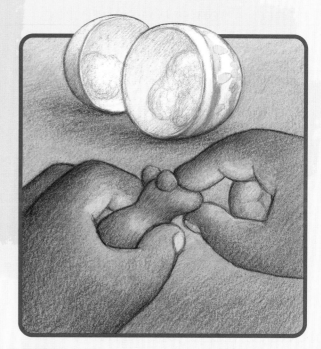

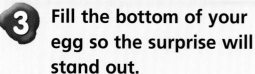 Fill the bottom of your egg so the surprise will stand out.

4 Use clay to make a tiny surprise. Place the surprise in your egg and close it.

Think Like an Artist

Surprise a friend by opening your egg.
Tell how the design on the outside of your
egg gives emphasis to the surprise inside.

Puppets

When Hua Hua Zhang was a child, she liked to sing and dance. Then she went to the Arts Academy in Beijing. There she learned a new way to share her ideas. She learned to use puppets!

Being a puppeteer can be hard work. Zhang writes her own stories. She makes puppets to share the stories. Then she rehearses until everything is just right.

Hua Hua Zhang

Materials Hua Hua Zhang uses in her art.

How does Hua Hua Zhang share her ideas?

Hua Hua Zhang loves her job. Every day is different. She gets to travel to new places. She gets to meet new people. Her art makes her happy. She likes using her art to make others happy too.

Make a Foil Relief

A relief design stands out from its background. Make a large foil relief design. Let it be a plan for small jewelry.

1 Cut out a large simple shape.

2 Glue scraps to your shape.

3 Glue your shape onto a cardboard square.

4 Cover the square with foil. Press it with your fingers to make the shapes and scraps stand out.

Look at some foil relief jewelry
designs other children made.

Cole, Age 7. *Foil Shapes.*
Cardboard and foil.

Adriana, Age 7. *Heart Design.*
Cardboard and foil.

Share Your Art

1. Who would wear your jewelry?
   Why would they like it?
2. Where did you show emphasis?

Unit Review

Think About Art

Match the art words with the pictures.

realistic   **pendant**   **mural**

jewelry   **public sculpture**   **symbol**

Write About Art

Write a description of an interesting stamp that you have seen. Describe its size, shape, color, and design. Tell what the design stands for.

Talk About Art

- Choose an artwork of yours that you could use as a book illustration.
- Think like a book designer. Describe the page where the artwork would appear.

Christo and Jeanne-Claude. *Running Fence, Sonoma and Marin Counties, California,*
1972–1976. Woven nylon fabric, stretched between steel poles, supported by steel cables,
18 feet by 24 ½ miles. © 1976 Christo. Photograph by Jeanne-Claude.

Put It All Together

1. Is this public sculpture a miniature or
   a large artwork? How can you tell?
2. Where is the emphasis in this sculpture?
3. Do you think this sculpture is a symbol
   of something? What?
4. Do you think *Running Fence* is a good
   title? Why or why not?

David Bates. *The Whittler,* 1983. Oil on canvas, 96 by 78 inches. Jack S. Blanton Museum of Art, The University of Texas at Austin, Michener Collection Acquisition Fund, 1983. ©David Bates. Photograph by George Holmes.

Types of Artworks

You have seen many types of artworks in this book. It is filled with paintings, sculptures, prints, and more. Look at the artwork on page 186. What type of artwork is it?

Artists use different materials to make their artworks. What materials do you think were used for *The Whittler?* What materials have you used to make art?

Meet the Artist

David Bates was born in Texas in 1952. His first works were paintings, such as *The Whittler.* Now Bates is a sculptor who works with wood, wire, and other materials. Bates says his artworks tell stories. What story do you think *The Whittler* tells? Find another artwork by Bates in this unit.

Weaving

This basket is useful art. It can hold many things. The artist made the basket by **weaving.** The artist wove stiff strips of birch bark over and under each other to bind them. Weaving gives the basket texture and pattern.

Artist unknown, Inupiat culture. *Birch Basket.*
Woven birch. Private collection.

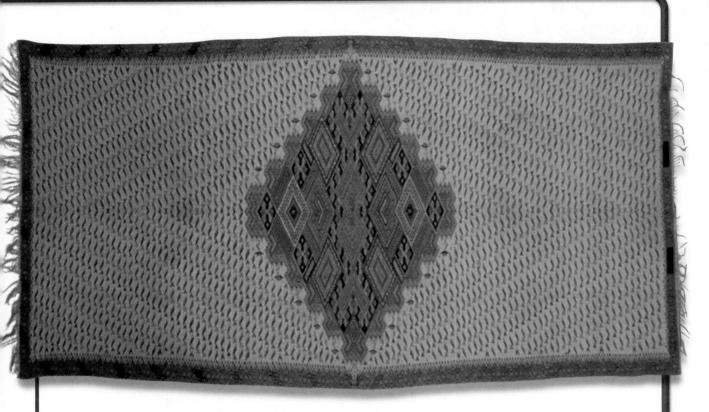

Artist unknown, Mexican. *Serape,* mid-19th century. Wool weft, cotton warp, silk, metallic thread, natural dyes. Fred Harvey Collection of the International Folk Art Foundation at the Museum of International Folk Art, Santa Fe, NM.

This artwork is called a serape. A serape is a soft blanket made of **fabric,** or cloth. The artist made the fabric by weaving thread or yarn. The artist used a **loom.** A loom is a weaving tool. It helps artists hold threads in place as they work. How are the two woven artworks alike? How are they different?

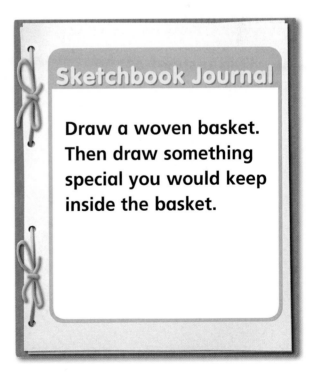

Sketchbook Journal

Draw a woven basket. Then draw something special you would keep inside the basket.

Studio 1

Weave Paper

Try your hand at weaving. Weave a paper artwork.

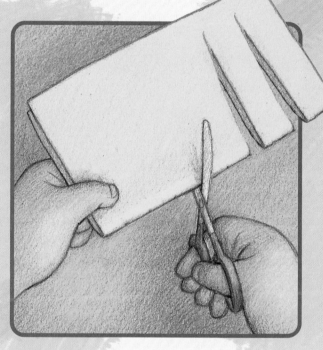

1 Fold a sheet of paper in half.

2 Cut lines across the fold. Stop about an inch from the edge.

Technique Tip

You can weave a pencil through the cuts to make space for the paper strip. Leave the pencil in place as you weave the strip.

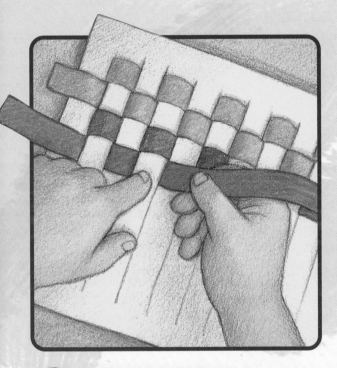

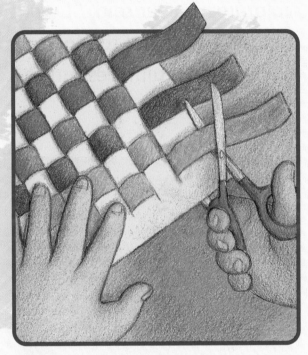

3 Weave a paper strip over and under. On the next row, go under and over.

4 When you finish weaving, trim the ends and glue them.

Think Like an Artist

Tell how you decided which colors to use.

More Fun with Sculpture

Alexander Calder made both of these sculptures. Calder said, "I want to make things that are fun to look at." What makes these sculptures fun to look at?

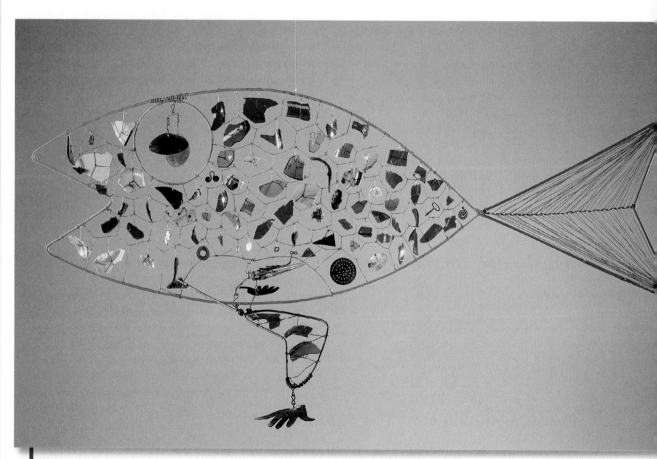

Alexander Calder. *Finny Fish,* 1948. Painted steel rod, wire, glass, and objects, 26 by 60 inches. National Gallery of Art, Washington, D.C.

Alexander Calder. *Big Bird,* 1937. Sheet metal, bolts, and paint, 88 by 50 by 59 inches . Private collection.

A material that an artist uses is called a **medium.** More than one medium is called **media.** These artworks were made from different media. The fish was made from wire and glass. The bird was made from sheet metal.

Calder had his own **style.** Style is an artist's special way of making art. How would you describe it?

Art Fact

Calder could find materials for making sculptures anywhere. At dinner one night, he sculpted a chicken from bread and a hairpin.

Make a Wire Sculpture

Follow these steps to make a sculpture
with wire.

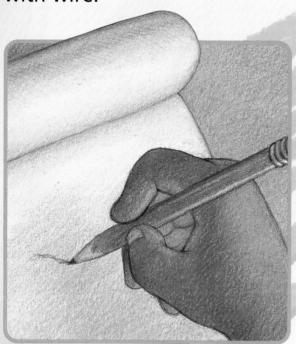

1 Draw a plan for
a wire sculpture.

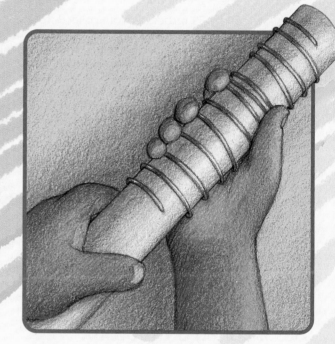

2 Get some wire. Bend it,
twist it, and curl it.

Technique Tip

One way to shape wire is to bend it or curl it
around a block or a pencil. Press the wire
against the object. Then slide the object out.

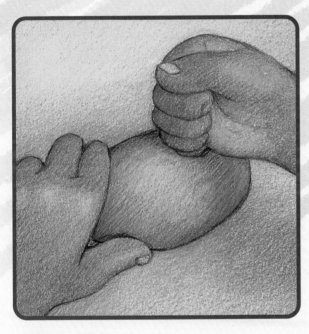

3 Make a base from clay. Carve the name of your sculpture on the base.

4 Add your wires to the base. Then carve your name in it.

Roller Coaster

Think Like an Artist

Compare your sculpture with others.

Explain how your sculpture is different.

Describe your style.

Celebrate with Art

Some artists make artworks for celebrations.
This artwork is a **headdress.** A headdress
is like a hat with decorations. When might
a person wear this headdress?

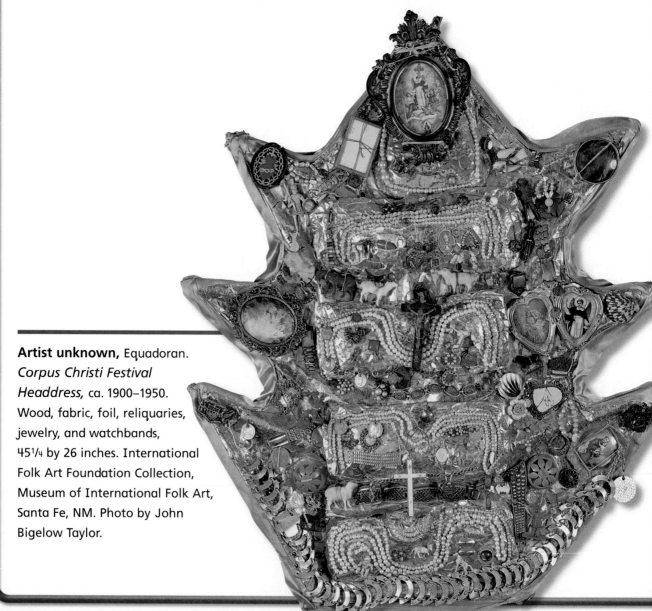

Artist unknown, Equadoran.
*Corpus Christi Festival
Headdress,* ca. 1900–1950.
Wood, fabric, foil, reliquaries,
jewelry, and watchbands,
45¼ by 26 inches. International
Folk Art Foundation Collection,
Museum of International Folk Art,
Santa Fe, NM. Photo by John
Bigelow Taylor.

Bamgboye. *Epa Headdress,* 1920. Carved polychrome wood, height 55 inches. Collection of The Newark Museum, Newark, NJ.

Headdresses have special meanings. The Yoruba people in Africa used this headdress in a festival many years ago. It celebrated the roles of the people.

Objects people used long ago are called **artifacts.** They were made to be used. Over time, people have come to see them as art.

Art in My World

Draw people at a celebration. Draw a headdress on each person.

197

Make a Headdress

Celebrate! Make and wear a special headdress.

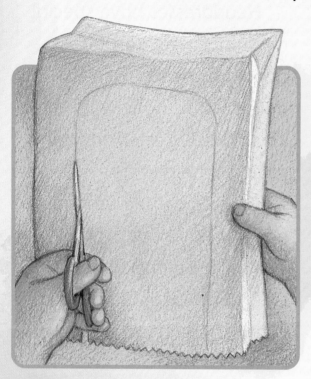

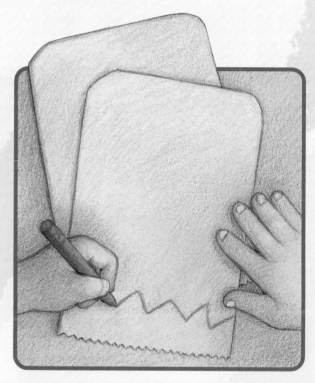

1 Draw and cut out two large U-shapes. Make them the same size.

2 Decorate the cutouts with different types of lines.

Technique Tip

Staple one side of the headdress. Then hold it on your head while your teacher staples the other side to make it fit.

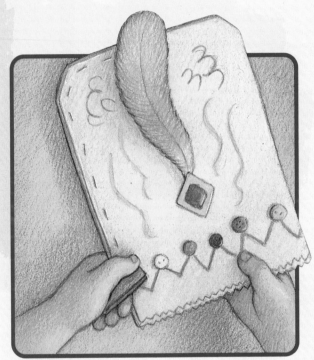

3 Glue on feathers, buttons, and other found materials.

4 Staple together the front and back along the sides.

Think Like an Artist

Tell why you decorated your headdress in the way that you did. Describe a celebration where you would wear it.

Media in Artworks

David Bates. *Feeding the Dogs,* 1986. Oil on canvas. 90¹/₁₆ by 67 inches. Collection of Phoenix Art Museum, Phoenix, AZ. Museum purchase.

What animal do you see in these artworks? The subjects are similar, but the artists used different media and have different styles.

William Wegman.
Cinderella, 1992.
Unique Polacolor ER
photograph, 20 by 24
inches. © William
Wegman. From the
book *Cinderella,*
Hyperion Books for
Children, New York,
1993.

What medium did each artist use? How does the media change the way the subjects look? Which artwork shows more details? Tell what you think the artists were trying to say.

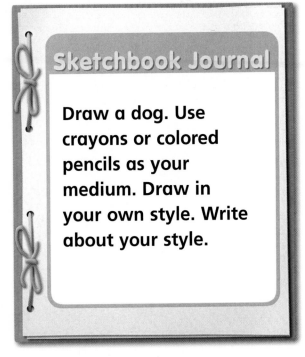

Sketchbook Journal

Draw a dog. Use crayons or colored pencils as your medium. Draw in your own style. Write about your style.

Masks for Expression

Have you ever worn a **mask** during a celebration? A mask hides your face and lets you express an idea. This mask shows a bear. What idea do you think the mask expresses?

Artist unknown, Eskimo (Yupik). *Mask: Bear Spirit,* late 19th century. Wood, paint, fiber, gut cord. Dallas Museum of Art, Dallas, TX. Gift of Elizabeth H. Penn. 1976.49.

Artist unknown, Aztec. *Mask Representing Chalchihuitlicue, "Lady Precious Green."* Wood inlaid with shell and turquoise. Museo Preistorico ed Etnografico Luigi Pigorini, Rome, Italy.

The mask on this page shows an Aztec goddess. It was made in Mexico.

Both masks were made in different places and long ago. Today, artists from all over the world make masks that express ideas about their culture.

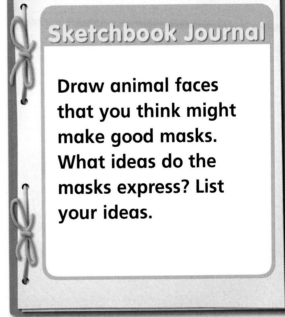

Sketchbook Journal

Draw animal faces that you think might make good masks. What ideas do the masks express? List your ideas.

Make a Sack Mask

Make a special mask to express yourself.

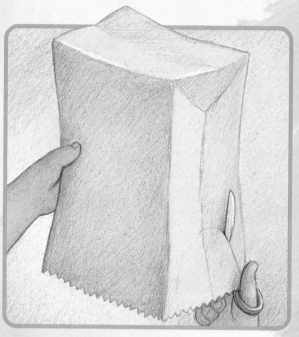

1 Cut shoulder curves in the sides of a sack.

2 Try on the sack. Ask a friend to mark the eyes.

Technique Tip

Be very careful when marking the eyeholes.
Press gently and draw circles around the eyes.

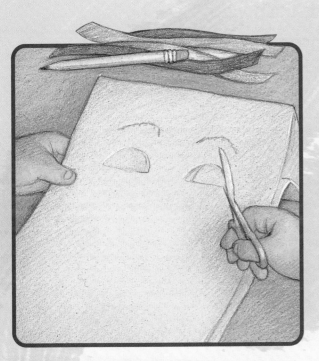

3 Take off the bag. Cut out shapes for the eyes.

4 Cut, curl, fold, and twist paper. Add details with line, shape, and color.

Think Like an Artist

Suppose someone finds your mask years from now. Explain what people might learn about your culture by looking at your mask.

Community Art

What might you call this artwork? This **art car** is an example of folk art. Each year Houston, Texas, has an art car parade. What kinds of fun artworks are in your community?

Colleena Hake and Phillip Estrada. *The Doll Car,* 1994. Automobile with plastic dolls and mixed media.

Keith Haring. *We the Youth,* 1987. Mural, approximately 100 by 30 feet (at tallest point). Philadelphia, PA.

This mural is a large artwork. It was painted on a wall in a community in Pennsylvania. The mural has a **theme.** A theme is a big idea, such as love or beauty. Artists express ideas about themes in different ways. What do you think is the theme of this mural?

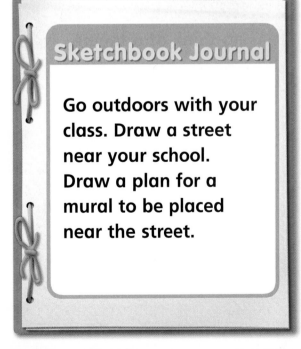

Sketchbook Journal

Go outdoors with your class. Draw a street near your school. Draw a plan for a mural to be placed near the street.

Make an Art Train

Decorate a train car. Make an art train with your class.

1 Work with your class to think of a theme.

2 Choose a box to use as a train car. Paint the box a bright color.

Technique Tip

Fill your box with packing peanuts or blocks while you work. The filler will keep the sides from bending in when you press on them.

3 Add designs and glue objects onto the box to fit the theme.

4 Put the cars together to make a model, or small copy, of a train.

Think Like an Artist

Tell how your decorations fit the theme.
Talk about each artist's part in making
the model.

Artists Make Quilts

A **quilt** is made of several layers of fabric. The top layer has fabric **quilt blocks** that are sewn together. Some quilts cover beds. Others hang on walls.

Artist unknown. *Sampler Block Quilt,* 1905.
Smithsonian American Art Museum, Washington, D.C.

Katherine Westphal. *Unveiling of the Statue of Liberty (After Edward Moran),* 1964. Batiked, quilted, and embroidered fabric, 92¾ by 66½ inches. Smithsonian American Art Museum, Washington, D.C.

Some quilts have a theme. A quilt's theme might come from fabric scraps that were cut from special clothing or material. Or, a quilt might show a theme in its design. What theme does this quilt show? Hint: look at the symbol in the center.

Research

Find other symbols of the United States or your community. Plan how you would show them in quilt blocks.

Studio 6

Make a Class Quilt

Work with your classmates to choose a theme for a class quilt. Make the quilt together.

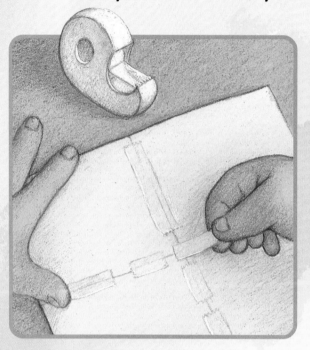

1 Tape four paper squares together to make a quilt block.

2 Draw symbols or a scene to fit the theme.

Technique Tip

You can draw four pictures, one in each small square. Or, you can draw one large picture across the entire quilt block.

3 Fill in the shapes with color.

4 Attach your block to the bulletin board with the others.

Think Like an Artist

Tell why the different quilt blocks work well together.

Jewelry

Mario Chavez chose his life's work when he was only fourteen years old. That is when he took his first jewelry class. Later he learned more by working for skilled jewelry makers.

Chavez creates jewelry that makes him happy. First, he draws a design. Then, he melts gold and silver. He shapes the metals and adds stones, such as diamonds or sapphires. Sometimes he uses strange objects instead. He has even used old coins and bones!

Mario Chavez creates art that you can wear.

Mario Chavez. *Past, Present, and Future; Grecian Sea; Pearl Island;* 2002. 22K gold and diamonds; 18 and 22K gold, Ancient Greek coin, and blue Austrailian opal; platinum and 22K gold, diamond, and South Sea pearl. Photograph © Alison Watson.

Chavez has fun with his work and hopes that his customers will enjoy his jewelry so much that they hand it down to their children. Chavez wants his artworks to last a long time.

Make a Woven Bookmark

Make a special artwork that is useful. Weave a bookmark.

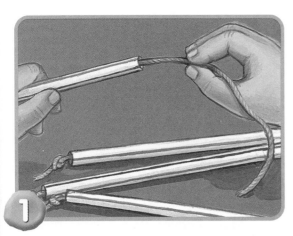

1 Push five strips of yarn through five drinking straws. Tie a knot in one end of each yarn strip.

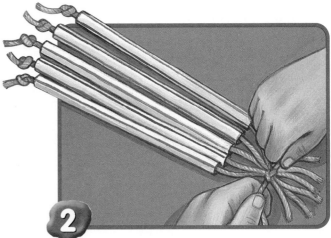

2 Tie the other ends of the yarn strips together.

3 Weave over and under the straws. Weave back and forth. Do it again and again.

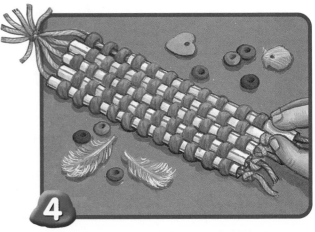

4 Cut the small knots. Pull out the straws. Tie the loose ends. Then add beads or other decorations.

How would you describe the patterns in these woven bookmarks by other children?

Chandler, Age 7.
Smiley Bookmark.
Yarn, sequins, and beads.

Carissa, Age 8.
Flag Bookmark.
Yarn, sequins, and beads.

Share Your Art

1. Explain how to weave.
2. Describe a problem you had. Tell how you solved it.

Think About Art

Match each word to a picture.

art car   fabric   model

artifact   mask   quilt

Artist unknown.
Pende Mbuyu Initiation Mask.

Write About Art

Think about all the art projects that you have made. Then write a plan for a new project that you would enjoy making. Tell what media and style you would use. Tell the theme.

Talk About Art

- Tell about the kind of artist you want to be.
- What media do you most enjoy working with?
- What themes will your artworks express?

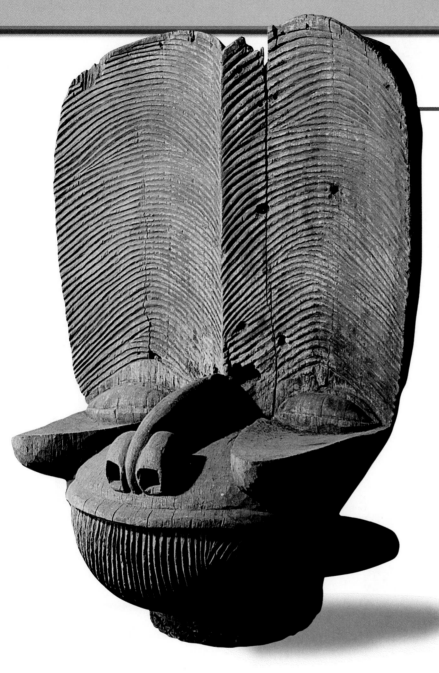

Put It All Together

1. What materials did the artist use?
2. How does the headdress show balance?
3. Why do you think the artist made the headdress?
4. Where and when might you wear this headdress?

Line

straight

curved

zigzag

thin

thick

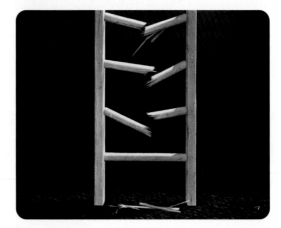
broken

Color

cool

warm

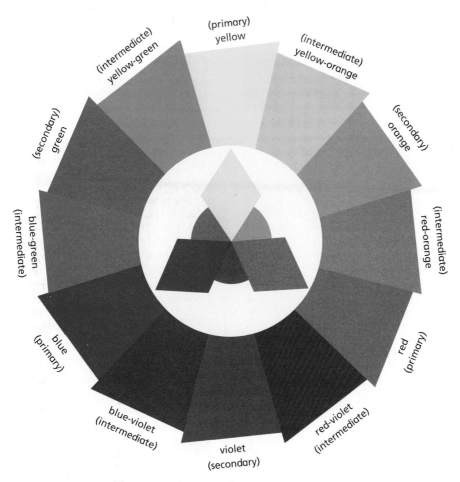

color wheel

Value

Shape

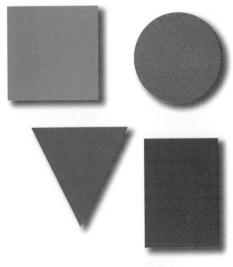

geometric shapes | organic shapes

Texture

bumpy

soft

shiny

prickly

sticky

fluffy

Form

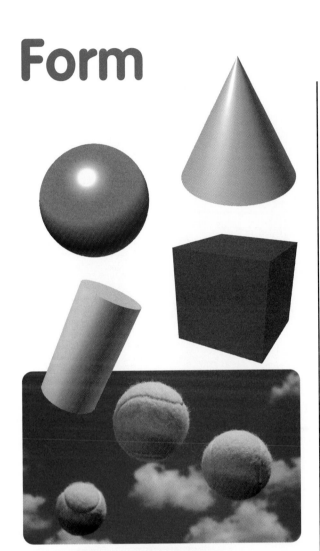

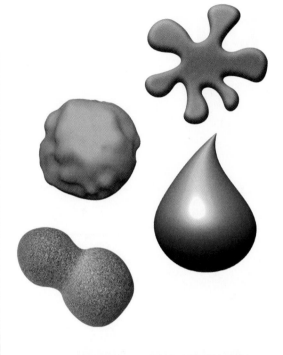

geometric forms | **organic forms**

225

Space

positive space

negative space

Principles of Design

Unity

Variety

Emphasis

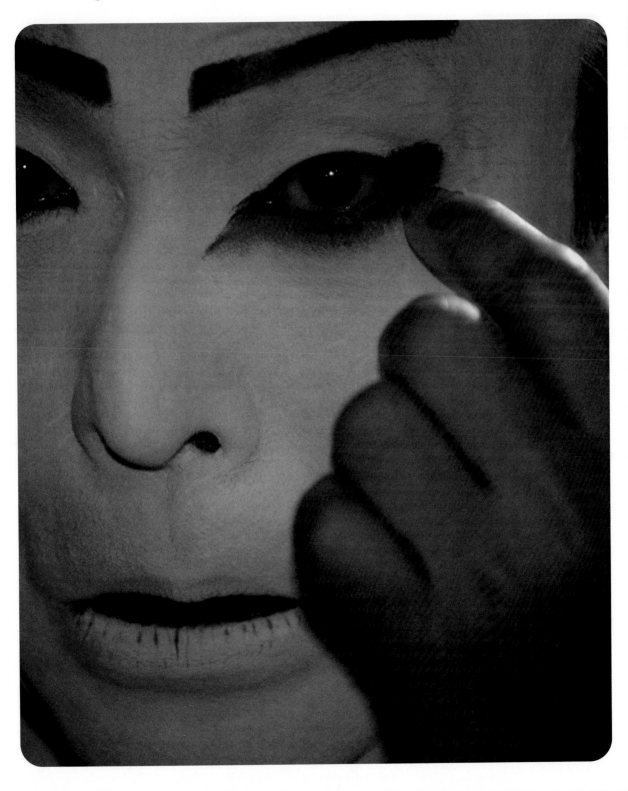

Principles of Design

Balance

Proportion

Principles of Design

Pattern

Rhythm

Think Safety

Read these safety rules. Be sure to follow these rules when you create artworks.

1. Keep art materials away from your mouth.

2. Keep art materials away from your eyes.

3. Do not breathe chalk dust or art sprays.

4. Look for the word *nontoxic* on labels. This means the materials are safe to use.

5. Always use safety scissors. Take care with all sharp objects.

6. Use only unused meat trays and egg cartons.

7. Wash your hands when you finish an artwork.

8. Get help from your teacher if you have a problem.

Can you think of more ways to be safe?

List of Artists

Unknown Artists

Artists

List of Artists

Picture Glossary

abstract
page 61

architecture
page 86

art car
page 206

Colleena Hake and Phillip Estrada.
The Doll Car, 1994.

artifact
page 197

Artist unknown. *Acoma Polychrome Jar*, ca. 1900.

asymmetrical balance
page 125

Artist unknown. *Inlay of a king or deity.* ca. 305-200 B.C.

B

balance
page 124

238

book designer
page 172

clay
page 109

close up
page 139

carve
page 101

D

design
page 91

E

ceramic
page 121

emphasis
page 169

expression
page 66

form
page 87

 F

fabric
page 189

 H

headdress
page 196

far away
page 139

 I

imaginary
page 159

Still from the animated feature *Monsters, Inc.*

intermediate colors
page 37

J
jewelry
page 168

Artist unknown. Berber Necklace.

K
kiln
page 109

L
landscape
page 74

lines
page 18

loom
page 189

M
mask
page 202

Artist unknown. Mask Representing Chalchihuitlicue.

medium
page 193

241

miniature
page 176

model
page 209

mood
page 40

mosaic
page 143

Artist unknown. Double-Headed Serpent.
A.D. 15th century.

motion
page 129

movement
page 128

mural
page 158

N

negative space
page 95

prints
page 53

proportion
page 139

public sculpture
page 155

Alexander Calder. *Red Horse*, 1974.

puppet
page 104

puppeteer
page 104

Q

quilt
page 210

Artist unknown. *Sampler Block Quilt*, 1905.

quilt block
page 210

R

radial balance
page 125

realistic
page 60

Rosa Bonheur. *The King of the Desert*, 19th century.

rhythm
page 128

S

sculpture
page 85

Edgar Degas. *The Little Fourteen-Year-Old Dancer,* 19th–20th century (executed ca. 1880; cast in 1922).

self-portrait
page 67

Mary Cassatt. *Self-Portrait,* ca. 1880.

shade
page 71

shapes
page 22

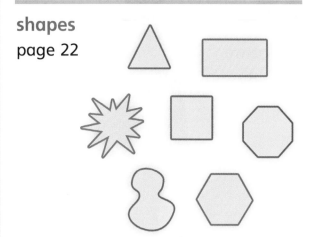

slab
page 121

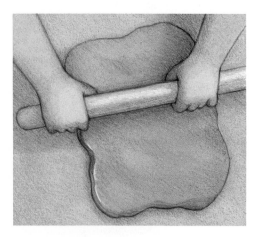

space
page 94

stencil print
page 57

still life
page 70

style
page 56

Franz Marc. *The Tiger*, 1913.

tint
page 71

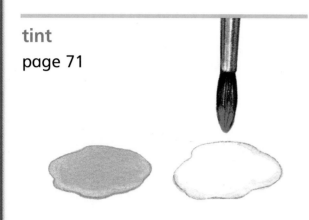

tradebeads
page 168

unity
page 135

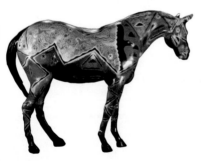

Bill Rabbit. Earth, Wind, and Fire, 2003.

variety
page 135

Joel Nakamura. Thunderbird Suite, 2001.

visual texture
page 32

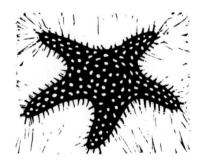

warm colors
page 41

Index

Index

Acknowledgments

ILLUSTRATIONS
20, 21, 24, 25, 28, 29, 34, 35, 38, 39, 42, 43, 54, 55, 58, 59, 62, 63, 68, 69, 72, 73, 76, 77, 88, 89, 92, 93, 96, 97, 102, 103, 106, 107, 110, 111, 122, 123, 126, 127, 130, 131, 136, 137, 140, 141, 144, 145, 156, 157, 160, 161, 164, 165, 168, 170, 171, 174, 175, 178, 179, 190, 191, 194, 195, 198, 199, 204, 205, 208, 209, 212, 213, 239(cr), 244, 246, 248(cl) Renee Graef

46, 80, 114, 148, 182, 216 Linda Hill Griffith

239(br), 245, 248(tl) Anni Matsick

241, 242, 247 Meredith Johnson

PHOTOGRAPHS

Every effort has been made to secure permission and provide appropriate credit for photographic material. The publisher deeply regrets any omission and pledges to correct errors called to its attention in subsequent editions.

Unless otherwise acknowledged, all photographs are the property of Scott Foresman, a division of Pearson Education.

Photo locators denoted as follows: Top (t), Center (c), Bottom (b), Left (l), Right (r), Background (Bkgd)

Front Matter
Page iv(bl), Gift of Mr. and Mrs. Charles Zadok. 195.1952. Digital image © The Museum of Modern Art/Licensed by Scala/Art Resource, NY. © 2004 Andre Dérain/Artists Rights Society (ARS), NY; 2(bl), Réunion des Musées Nationaux/Art Resource, NY. © 2004 Estate of Pablo Picasso/Artists Rights Society (ARS), New York; 2(br), National Gallery of Art, Washington, D.C. Gift of the W. L. and May T. Mellon Foundation. Photograph by Bob Grove, © 1998 Board of Trustees, National Gallery of Art, Washington; 4(b), © Roy King/SuperStock; 5(t), © Smithsonian American Art Museum, Washington, D.C./Art Resource, NY; 7(tl), National Museum of American Art, Smithsonian Institution, Washington, D.C./Art Resource, NY; 7(tr), Scala/Art Resource, NY. © Henry Moore Foundation; 7(b), Malcah Zeldis/Art Resource, NY; 10, Reproduction © Musée des Beaux-Arts de Bordeaux; 14, © Réunion des Musées Nationaux/Art Resource, NY.

Units 1–6
Page 17, Mary Cassatt. Self-Portrait, ca. 1880. Watercolor on paper, 13 by 9 5/8 inches. © The National Portrait Gallery, Smithsonian Institution. Art Resource, New York; 17(bc), © C Squared Studios/Getty Images; 18, © Historical Picture Archive/ Corbis; 22, Sidney and Harriet Janis Collection Fund, and gift of Suzy Prudden and Joan H. Meijer, in memory of F.H. Hirschland. Digital image © The Museum of Modern Art/Licensed by Scala/Art Resource, NY. © 2004 Paul Klee/Artists Rights Society (ARS), New York; 27, © Digital Stock; 27, © Corbis; 27, © Getty Images; 27, © Michael and Patricia Fogden/Corbis; 30, Gift of Mr. and Mrs. Charles Zadok. 195.1952. Digital image © The Museum of Modern Art/Licensed by Scala/Art Resource, NY. © 2004 Andre Dérain/Artists Rights Society (ARS), NY; 31, © National Gallery of Art, Washington, D.C./SuperStock; 33, © Winifred Wisniewski; Frank Lane Pictures/Corbis; 36, Hirshhorn Museum and Sculpture Garden, Smithsonian Institution, Gift of Joseph H. Hirshhorn, 1966 (66.3189). Photo by Lee Stalsworth; 40, © Janet Fish/Licensed by VAGA, New York, NY; 41(b), © MedRes/Getty Images; 48, © Getty Images; 48, © Getty Images; 48, © Getty Images; 49, © 2004 Artists Rights Society (ARS), New York/ADAGP, Paris; 50, © Réunion des Musées Nationaux/Art Resource, NY. © Estate of Fernand Léger/Artists Rights Society (ARS), NY; 51, © Bettmann/ Corbis; 57(r), © Gary W. Carter/Corbis; 60, National Gallery of Art, Washington, D.C. Woodner Collection, 1991.182.5. Image © 2003 Board of Trustees, National Gallery of Art, Washington, D.C.; 61, Städtische Galerie Im Lenbachhaus, Munich; 64, Digital image © The Museum of Modern Art/Licensed by Scala/Art Resource, NY. © Estate of Fernand Léger/Artists Rights Society (ARS), NY; 66, © Smithsonian American Art Museum, Washington, D.C. / Art Resource, NY; 67, Estate of Alice Neel/Courtesy Robert Miller Gallery, New York; 70, © Musée d'Orsay, Paris/SuperStock; 71, © 1996 Artists Rights Society (ARS), New York/VG Bild-Kunst, Bonn. Photograph by Elke Walford; 74, © Giraudon/Art Resource, NY; 78, © Corbis; 82, © Jose Luis Pelaez, Inc./Corbis; 82, © SuperStock; 85(bl), Photograph © Davis Mather, Santa Fe, NM; 86(t), © World Travel Images; 86(br), Richard Cummins/Corbis; 90, © David Young-Wolff/PhotoEdit; 94, Réunion des Musées Nationaux/Art Resource, NY. © 2004 Estate of Pablo Picasso/Artists Rights Society (ARS), New York; 95(b), © Lauros/Giraudon/Bridgemans Art Library; 95(t), © ART on FILE/Corbis. © Deborah Butterfield; 98, © Smithsonian American Art Museum, Washington, D.C./Art Resource, NY; 100, Photo by: John Bigelow Taylor/ Museum of International Folk Art, Santa Fe, NM; 101(t), Museum of International Folk Art, Santa Fe, NM; 108, John Bigelow Taylor/Eugene and Claire Bigelow Collection, Fenimore Art Museum/Art Resource, NY; 109, Crizmac; 112(tr), © James Mason/ Photo courtesy of the Columbus Cultural Art Center; 113, Photo courtesy of the Columbus Cultural Art Center; 116, © Lon C. Diehn/PhotoEdit; 116, © Omni Photo/Index Stock Imagery; 116, © Dale O'Dell/Corbis; 117, Collection of Whitney Museum of

Acknowledgments

American Art. Purchase, with funds from the Louis and Bessie Adler Foundation, Inc., Seymour M. Klein, President, the Gilman Foundation, Inc., the Howard and Jean Lipman Foundation, Inc., and the National Endowment for the Arts, 79.4. Photograph © 1996, Whitney Museum of American Art; 118, © Erich Lessing/Art Resource, New York; 119(l), Charles Emile Carolus-Duran. Painter Edouard Manet, ca. 1880. Oil on canvas, 25 1/3 by 21 inches. Musée d'Orsay, Paris, France. © Erich Lessing/Art Resource, NY; 120, © Royal Ontario Museum/Corbis; 121, © Werner Foreman/Art Resource, NY; 125, Charles Edwin Wilbour Fund, 49.61.1-4/ Brooklyn Museum of Art; 125,© Peter Dazeley/Getty Images; 128, Musée d'Orsay, Paris/SuperStock; 129, © Paul A. Souders/ Corbis; 129, © Getty Images; 132, © World Films Enterprise/Corbis; 133, National Gallery of Art, Washington, D.C. Gift of the W. L. and May T. Mellon Foundation. Photograph by Bob Grove, © 1998 Board of Trustees, National Gallery of Art, Washington; 139, © Christie's Images/SuperStock. © 2004 Artists Rights Society (ARS), New York/ADAGP, Paris; 146(tr), Maribeth Koutrakos; 147, Maribeth Koutrakos; 150, © Corbis; 150, © Lisa Berkshire/Getty Images; 152, Gift of Mr. and Mrs. Klaus G. Perls/Image ©2003 Board of Trustees, National Gallery of Art, Washington; 153(br), © Hulton-Deutsch Collection/Corbis; 153, © The Studio Dog/Getty Images; 153, © Getty Images; 153, © Getty Images; 153, © ThinkStock/SuperStock; 155, © Art on File/Corbis. © Claes Oldenburg and Coosje van Bruggen; 158, © Roy King/SuperStock; 159, © Jeffry W. Myers/Corbis; 162, 163(l), 163(r), Trademarks and copyrights used herein are properties of the United States Postal Service and are used under license to Scott Foresman. All rights reserved; 166, 167, © Art Resource, NY. © 2004 Estate of Alexander Calder/Artists Rights Society (ARS), New York; 168, © Francesco Venturi; Kea Publishing Service/Corbis; 180(tr), © Andrew B. Duvall III; 180(br), © David H. Wells/Corbis; 181, Richard Termine; 184, © SuperStock; 184, © Lindsay Hebberd/Corbis; 184, © Archivo Iconografico, S.A./Corbis; 187(b), © Weinberg/Clark/ Getty Images; 187, Photograph by Lee Clockman, courtesy of Gerald Peters Gallery; 88, © Pat O'Hara/Corbis; 189, Fred Harvey Collection of the International Folk Art Foundation, Photo by: Blair Clark/Museum of International Folk Art, Santa Fe, NM; 192, National Gallery of Art, Washington, D.C. Gift of Mr. and Mrs. Klaus G. Perls. © 2004 Estate of Alexander Calder/Artists Rights Society (ARS), New York; 193, © Art Resource, NY. © 2004 Estate of Alexander Calder/Artists Rights Society (ARS), New York; 196, Photo by: John Bigelow Taylor/ Museum of International Folk Art Foundation/Museum of International Folk Art, Santa Fe, NM; 197, © The Newark Museum/Art Resource, NY; 200, Collection of Phoenix Art Museum, Museum purchase; 201, *Untitled*, 1991 (from *Cinderella*, Hyperion). Color Poloroid, 24 by 20 inches/William Wegman; 203, © Werner Foreman/Corbis; 206, © Colleena Hake and Phillip Estrada. Photo © Harrod Blank Photography; 207, Photograph © Michael LoFurno/Composite, Inc.; 210, © Smithsonian American Art Museum, Washington, D.C./Art Resource, NY; 211, © Smithsonian American Art Museum, Washington, D.C./Art Resource, NY; 214(tr), Alison Watson Photography; 215(t), Alison Watson Photography; 218(cl), © Jonathan Blair/Corbis; 219(c), © Bowers Museum of Cultural Art/Corbis; 219, © Werner Foreman/Art Resource, New York.

Back Matter
Page 220, © Getty Images; 220, © Corbis; 220, © Getty Images; 221, © Getty Images; 221, © digitalvisiononline.com; 222, © Darrell Gulin/Corbis; 222, © Eric Crichton/Corbis; 223, © Paul Chauncey/Corbis; 223, © Corbis; 223, © Pat Doyle/Corbis; 224, © Robert Yin/Corbis; 224, © David Frazier/© Corbis; 224, © Peter Dazeley/Corbis; 224, © Richard Hamilton Smith/Corbis; 224, © Charles Gold/Corbis; 224, © Lance Nelson/Corbis; 225, © The Purcell Team/Corbis; 225, © Lindsey P. Martin/Corbis; 225, © Nik Wheeler/Corbis; 227, © Randy Faris/Corbis; 228, © Bob Krist/Corbis; 229, © Charles & Josette Lenars/Corbis; 230, © Mark Gibson/ Corbis; 231, © Tom Bean/Corbis; 232, © Corbis; 233, © Getty Images; 238 (tl) © Burnstein Collection/Corbis; 238 (cl) © Alan Schein Photography/Corbis; 238 (bl) © Harrod Blank; 238 (tr) © 1993 Sotheby's, inc.; 238 (cr) © Charles Edwin Wibour Fund, 49.61.1-4/Brooklyn Museum of Art.; 238 (br) © Dave Bartruff/Corbis; 239 (tl) © Old School Photo; 239 (tl) © Jimmy Johnson/The Image Bank/Getty Images; 239 (cl) © Lon C. Diehn/Photo Edit; 239 (bl) © Corbis; 239 (tr) © Omni Photo Communications Inc./ Index Stock Imagery; 239 (cr) © Gary W. Carter/Corbis; 240 (cl) © ThinkStock/Getty Images; 240 (bl) © Dave G. Houser/Corbis; 240 (cr) © R. W. Jones/Corbis; 240 (br), *Monsters Inc.*, Mike Wazowski and James P. Sullivan (2001), Pixar/Walt Disney Co., courtesy of the Everett Collection; 241 (cl) © Francesco Venturi; Kea Publishing Service/Corbis; 241 (cl) © Philip Gould/Corbis; 241 (tr) © David Samuel Robbins/Corbis; 241 (cr) "Lady Precious Green." Museo Preistorico ed Etno Grafico Luigi Pigorini, Rome, Italy.; 242 (tl) © Werner H Müller/Corbis; 242 (bl) © The British Museum, London; 242 (tr) © Chris Rogers/Corbis; 242 (cr) © David Robinson/Corbis; 242 (br) © ART on FILE/Corbis; 243 (cl)© Elio Ciol/Corbis; 243 (bl) © Alan Schein Photography/Corbis; 243 (tr) © Gianni Dagli Orti/Corbis; 244 (cl) © Dave Bartruff/Corbis; 244 (tr) Artist unknown, Burmese. *Puppets*, date unknown. Myanmar (Burma).; 244 (cr) © Omni Photo/Index Stock Imagery; 244 (br) © Smithsonian American Art Museum, Washington , D. C./Art Resource, NY; 245 (tl) © Corbis; 245(cl), Smithsonian American Art Museum, Washington, D.C./Art Resource, NY.; 245(tr), Christie's Images/SuperStock; 245(cr), The National Portrait Gallery, Smithsonian Institution, Washington, D.C./Art Resource, NY; 246 (bl) © Corbis; 246 (tr) © Stapleton Collection/Corbis; 246 (cr), © David Young-Wolff/PhotoEdit; 246(br), Städtische Galerie im Lenbachhaus, Munich, Germany.; 247 (cl) © Corbis; 247 (bl) © Museum of Anthropology at Xalapa, University of Veracruz, Mexico; 247 (tr) © Zeva Oelbaum/Corbis; 247 (br) © Phil Schermeister/Corbis; 248 (bl) © The Trail of Painted Ponies; 248 (cr) © Martha Paulos/Getty Images; 248 (br) © Corbis